COLON[IAL]
WILLIAMSBURG

Official Guidebook

Containing a brief History of the old City,
and of its Renewing, with Remarks on the
six chief Appeals thereof; and Descriptions
of near one hundred & fifty Dwelling-Houses,
Shops, & publick Buildings. *Completely
illustrated.* Also a large Guide-Map.

WILLIAMSBURG, VIRGINIA
1976

ISBN: 0-910412-32-4

Library of Congress Catalog Card No. 56–402
Printed in the United States of America

Table of Contents

A NOTE ON THE GUIDEBOOK

FOR your convenience in identifying buildings wherever you may find yourself in Williamsburg, the house histories in this Guidebook have been grouped by streets. Street names are arranged alphabetically and appear at the top of each page. The letter following a house name indicates the side of the street on which the building is located. A detailed map in the back of the Guidebook gives the names and locations of all the houses.

Because of their architectural, historical, or practical interest, a few buildings that do not fall within the area or period of restoration have been included in the Guidebook and on the map. Space has permitted the inclusion only of outbuildings conspicuously located.

AN INTRODUCTION TO WILLIAMSBURG

IF Henry Wetherburn, tavern-keeper of eighteenth-century Williamsburg, were to return to Colonial Williamsburg today, would he recognize his tavern and the town? Would Clementina Rind, the printer's widow who carried on the *Virginia Gazette* after her husband's death, still find Duke of Gloucester Street familiar? And how about James Lafayette, the slave who lived in Williamsburg as a spy for General Lafayette in the days leading up to Yorktown? Could he rediscover the outbuildings and dark attics that blacks frequented?

The answer to these questions must be a qualified yes. If Henry, Clementina, James, and their compatriots were to revisit their green country town today, they would recognize its general plan—broad Duke of Gloucester Street stretching nearly a mile from the College of William and Mary to the Capitol, the spacious Market Square and Palace greens, the houses set back precisely from the street, and the fences defining each lot. Most of the familiar landmarks would be there, including the Capitol, Gaol, Courthouse, Powder Magazine, Bruton Parish Church, Governor's Palace, and College.

But the paved streets, the brick sidewalks, the street lights, and the fire hydrants would be strange to eighteenth-century eyes, as would the curiously dressed thousands of visitors. The whole town would seem tidier than the former inhabitants remembered, with houses beter painted, greens more smoothly cropped, and gardens spruced up and adorned with more flowers. They would miss the dozens of saddle and draft horses and the variety of vehicles, especially the two-wheeled riding chairs; the cows, chickens, sheep, and other livestock in every part of town; the streets and paths mired with mud or deep in dust; and the clouds of flies and mosquitoes in summer. Perhaps most of all they would miss the pungent smells of animal manure, rooting hogs, backyard privies, and unwashed humanity.

Obviously Colonial Williamsburg has done much to preserve and restore the environment of the onetime capital of Virginia. It would be impossible to revert fully to the customs of the colonial period or to tolerate the lack of sanitation that prevailed. Moreover, the safety and comfort of hundreds of thousands of people who visit the town each year and of several hundred citizens who dwell within the Historic Area necessarily prevent the complete depiction of eighteenth-century conditions. By filling out the picture with explanations, demonstrations, publications, films, and other devices, Colonial Williamsburg hopes that visitors will better understand and appreciate the life and some of the aspirations of the men and women of that earlier Williamsburg.

The Six Appeals of Williamsburg

1. Architecture

The physical appearance of the major portion of a colonial town is instructive in itself. Francis Nicholson, the lieutenant governor from 1698 to 1705 who laid out the new capital of Williamsburg, was justifiably proud of his town plan. The 99-foot-wide central avenue formed the principal axis, crossed at a right angle by the stately approach to the Governor's Palace. Nicholson envisaged a country town with restful public greens and every house on the main street allotted at least a half-acre of land. Con-

forming setbacks, building heights, and fencing assured a pleasing orderliness, and the location of many important buildings and some modest homes emphasized both the structures and the vistas at the ends of streets.

Colonial fashions in architecture, as in dress, came from England, but, in the words of a contemporary, were "adapted to the Nature of the Country by the Gentlemen there." Alexander Spotswood, lieutenant governor from 1710 to 1722, employed geometry in designing several of the public buildings, and yet even the most elaborate structures were modified to meet local needs, the climate, and the building materials and labor skills available. The result was simple but subtle ornamentation and a scale that magnified, rather than dwarfed, the human figure.

Many public buildings and a few private dwellings and shops were of brick, made locally and laid in the prevailing fashions of Flemish and English bond. Most Williamsburg houses, however, were built of wood, which was far less costly and less susceptible to dampness. These frame houses were often painted white and usually had a steep-pitched A-roof, a gambrel roof, or a hip roof. A brick chimney was almost always placed at one end, and frequently at both. Outside shutters for frame houses and inside shutters for brick residences became increasingly common. Interior woodwork, including mantels, molded cornices, chair rails, and paneling, was normally painted.

Walls were usually of plaster, white-washed or occasionally papered.

To protect against fire, cooking odors, and heat in summer, the kitchen usually occupied a separate building situated a short distance from the house. The smokehouse, wellhead, and dairy customarily stood between the house and garden, with the privy, more obliquely known as the "necessary house," farther removed. In addition, there were usually a stable and coach house as well as a storehouse—then called a "lumber house." Slaves might dwell in some of these outbuildings.

The oldest of the public structures was the Wren Building of the College of William and Mary, erected between 1695 and 1700. It has stood ever since at the center of the College yard. When restoration of Williamsburg began, Bruton Parish Church and the President's House on the College grounds had maintained their functions continuously since colonial times; nearly the same can be said of the Courthouse of 1770 and the College's Brafferton Hall. Although variously employed, the Public Gaol, Magazine, and Public Records Office, too, had withstood the challenge of time. Of the prominent buildings only the Capitol, Palace, and Raleigh Tavern had to be reconstructed.

Eighteenth-century Williamsburg, then, was a carefully planned town with some of the handsomest public buildings to be found in the English colonies. In 1926, when the restoration started, the colonial town plan

was virtually intact, and 88 original buildings from the eighteenth and early nineteenth centuries survived. These old structures were carefully treated to insure their permanent preservation, and major buildings that had succumbed to fire, destruction, and decay were reconstructed after meticulous research had determined their former location and appearance.

2. Gardens and Greens

In a colonial country town like Williamsburg—despite being a planned city it was more rural than urban—nearly every family might raise vegetables, cultivate a few fruit trees and berry bushes, and keep domestic animals. A horse or two, a cow, and maybe some pigs and chickens would have been most common; some households could have added sheep, goats, ducks, and geese; other households perhaps a team of oxen.

Gardening activity thus fitted into the tight complex of domestic outbuildings and fenced plots typically found on the small town lot: stables, paddock, service yard, smokehouse, well, kitchen, orchard, and perhaps slave quarters. These, along with trees and plantings, help to recreate the landscape character of the colonial town. The grounds of the Governor's Palace, with their numerous outbuildings and comparatively elaborate gardens, plus a few other more or less extensive layouts, show the integrated organization of domestic function and natural beauty.

The abundance of unfamiliar plant species in the New World and the prevailing curiosity about natural history in the eighteenth century stimulated botanical interest. Men like John Custis of Williamsburg developed specimen gardens and exchanged plant materials and information with other plantsmen. Custis wrote a London friend: "I have a pretty little garden in which I take more satisfaction than in anything in this world and have a collection of tolerable good flowers and greens from England." In many Virginia gardens native trees, shrubs, flowers, and food plants shared space with specimens from abroad, usually imported as seeds or bulbs.

Although many traces were found in the ground, none of Williamsburg's eighteenth-century gardens survived intact into the twentieth; hence the designs of today's gardens have been derived largely from English precedents and from evidence relating to sites elsewhere in the southern colonies. Marl or brick paths linking associated buildings, and fences along property lines as required by colonial law, contribute to the geometry of this setting. Archaeological evidence, maps, written descriptions, and gardening books that might have influenced the concepts of Williamsburg residents assisted in the development of appropriate gardens. In the garden plantings, emphasis is placed on materials—both native and introduced—that could have been available to colonial households.

3. Furniture and Furnishings

More than 200 rooms in the 45 buildings open to the public add still another dimension to the setting, namely, typically and authentically furnished interiors. They range from the dreary cells of the Gaol, the simple quarters of cooks and coachmen, and the busy shops of the craftsmen to the

handsome living rooms of affluent merchants and lawyers and the impressive chambers of the Governor's Palace. The furnishings have come from many parts of the world, just as did similar articles in the eighteenth century. The guides and craftsmen also wear the clothing styles of that day.

English fashions determined the general style of American eighteenth-century household furnishings. In return for tobacco, British ports shipped to Virginia not only merchandise made in the United Kingdom but also occasional items of German,

Dutch, French, and Italian—or even Chinese and Indian—manufacture. Sea captains bought American-made "venture furniture" on speculation in New England and other northern ports for sale in the South. Many of the simpler furnishings were the work of Williamsburg craftsmen.

In assembling and installing appropriate eighteenth-century furnishings, Colonial Williamsburg curators have been guided by original inventories, by fragments excavated from building sites, and by colonial orders for merchandise to be sent over from England. Thus, when Governor Fauquier died at the Palace, an inventory of his possessions was made, and Governor Botetourt's executors prepared an itemized listing, room by room. Documentary and archaeological evidence together helped make possible an approach to historical fidelity, not only in furniture but also in fabrics, glass, china, and even such intimate details as the silver-rimmed spectacles beside an open book or playing cards laid out ready for a game.

Furnishing a cross section of a colonial American town with antique examples has enabled Colonial Williamsburg to acquire one of the most outstanding and comprehensive collections of seventeenth- and eighteenth-century American and English art materials in existence.

4. Crafts

Williamsburg in the eighteenth century was a small commercial center where some 50 hand crafts flourished. A few of them were carried on in the home; the women spun and wove cloth, and dipped or molded candles. Most crafts were performed by master craftsmen, journeymen, and apprentices laboring in shops or at building sites. They worked as housewrights, cabinetmakers, coopers, or basketmakers. They beat iron, raised silver, or founded brass, as well as fashioned guns, clocks, jewelry, or musical instruments. They ground

meal and baked bread, made boots or harness, dressed wigs, and conducted apothecary and millinery shops. An occasional traveling musician taught the music and instruments of the time.

Colonial Williamsburg has over 100 men and women serving as master craftsmen, journeymen, apprentices, and interpreters in a score of craft shops. In addition, half a dozen outdoor craft demonstrations are given when the season permits. In the costume of his eighteenth-century predecessor, each craftsman works with the sturdy tools of colonial days, fashioning articles of beauty, character, and utility. The busy, cluttered, and often noisy shops show much about the everyday life of "the middling sort," men and women who conducted respectable though small businesses. While machines and the assembly line have long since displaced most crafts in the manufacturing economy, the Williamsburg program helps assure the survival of these crafts as sources of historical knowledge and artistic satisfaction.

5. History and Heritage

The four appeals of Williamsburg listed above are all part of the social history of the colonial period. In addition, the restored town recalls important political principles of lasting importance to all men everywhere. Among them are:

The concept of the integrity of the individual. During the eighteenth century, man's respect for his fellow man grew. Philosophers and politicians alike shared a new awareness of the inherent dignity of every person. Thomas Jefferson best expressed this concept, although in actuality it was conspicuously limited, in Virginia as elsewhere, for slaves, women, debtors, and others. This appreciation of individual worth was fundamental in the struggle for freedom and self-government. It remains today the essential motive and goal of any free society, for, as Jefferson said, "The world belongs always to the living generation."

The concept of responsible leadership. Virginia's planter aristocracy,

trained to leadership from youth, accepted public obligations without question. The ruling class was composed of the larger plantation owners, merchants, and professional men. They willingly served as legislators

in Williamsburg, as justices of the peace, and as members of their own parish vestries, which had certain governmental duties. Washington, for example, conscientiously attended sessions of the House of Burgesses and meetings of the vestry of Truro Parish. These experiences of leadership in public affairs developed the generation of Virginia patriots who helped carry through the Revolution and launch the new republic.

The concept of self-government. From 1619, when the first representative assembly in America met at Jamestown, Virginians believed themselves capable of managing their own public affairs. They recognized the traditional overall authority of the crown, but resented any interference in their internal government by a distant Parliament. Thus Patrick Henry dared to speak heatedly against the Stamp Act at the Capitol in 1765. Ultimately, when legal and constitutional protest had failed to secure enough political autonomy to satisfy the Virginia leaders, they turned to independence. The struggle for self-government was thus a chief cause of the Revolution in Virginia.

The concept of individual liberty. Virginians believed that as British subjects they possessed important individual liberties and rights rooted in Magna Charta. Their efforts to protect these liberties culminated in the Virginia Declaration of Rights. This great document, drafted by George Mason and adopted unanimously in 1776 by legislators assembled at the Capitol in Williamsburg, asserted that "all men are by nature equally free and independent . . . when they enter into a state of society" (the latter clause excluded slaves). The Declaration's sixteen articles set forth fundamental rights such as free elections, trial by jury, freedom of the press, subordination of military to civil authority, and freedom of religion. The declaration inspired the first ten amendments to the Constitution of the United States and has influenced many subsequent bills of rights throughout the world.

The concept of opportunity. The colonization of Virginia is a chapter in the story of mankind's old dream of establishing a more abundant life in a new land. Those who undertook the hazardous and costly voyage—again except slaves—did so chiefly because they wanted a better chance for themselves and their children. Virginia offered a new measure of indi-

vidual and political freedom, a class structure less rigid than that of England, the opportunities of a growing colony, and the lure of cheap land and a frontier pushing westward.

6. Preservation Research

Visitors to Williamsburg often ask about what lies behind the work of restoration. The largely invisible foundation of what the visitor sees is research dedicated to sound preservation and restoration procedures. A skilled research group, including historians, architects, archaeologists, and curators, works constantly toward this end. Historical analysis at Williamsburg combines investigative techniques in each of these fields. A huge

volume of information has been accumulated from documentary sources; from excavations of foundations, abandoned wells, and trash pits; from exhaustive examinations of surviving colonial structures, both in the town and throughout the tidewater region; and from studies of countless examples of furnishings of the colonial period. Based on this research, films, publications, and lectures illuminate the processes of preservation.

Williamsburg Becomes the Capital

The site of Williamsburg was first settled in 1633 by hard-pressed colonists from nearby Jamestown as a stockaded outpost against Indian attack. By 1699 Middle Plantation, as it was called, consisted of several houses, two mills, a few shops, a small brick church, and the new and imposing building of the College of William and Mary. When the statehouse at Jamestown was leveled by fire, the legislators voted to move their capital to Middle Plantation, which they renamed Williamsburg in honor of King William III. Jamestown at that time was a cluttered little village all but surrounded by brackish swamps. Middle Plantation, located on a broad ridge between the York and James rivers, had access to both via navigable creeks but lay out of range of enemy warships.

Not long after Williamsburg became the capital, it also became the social and cultural as well as the political center of the entire Virginia colony. Here the royal governor lived, the General Assembly convened, and the courts sat. Twice each year, when the General Court was in session, crowds came to Williamsburg for "Publick Times." The population of the town (normally only about 1,800) doubled almost overnight. Shops were stocked with the latest goods imported from London as well as with the products of local craftsmen. There were horse races, fairs, and formal balls. Auctions were held at various taverns and on Market Square. For several weeks the city hummed with activity.

In Williamsburg's new H-shaped brick Capitol—the first statehouse in America to be so named—laws were passed affecting a vast territory that stretched westward to the Mississippi River. Virginia was the most populous of all the British colonies. Every person in the enormous domain was subject nominally to the government at Williamsburg—large planters and small freeholders in the Tidewater, the Piedmont, and the Shenandoah Valley; merchants and dock hands at the busy wharves in Hampton; settlers searching for pitch, tar, and turpentine in the Dismal Swamp on the North Carolina border; German immigrant ironworkers in Spotsylvania; tenants on Lord Fairfax's five million acres of the Northern Neck; and frontiersmen deep in Indian territory on the banks of the Ohio.

Williamsburg, however, was chiefly a planter's capital. The ruling class of the colony depended largely on the growth and sale of tobacco, the broad-leafed "Imperial weed" that John Rolfe had learned in 1612 could be raised in Virginia for the English market. Some of the planters lived in the Piedmont, rolling country beyond the fall line of the rivers, but most of the leaders of this aristocracy came from the Tidewater. Presiding over a plantation, which was a miniature village, the large planter lived most of the time in his mansion house, usually close by one of the many convenient waterways. A typical planter spent several weeks of the year in Williamsburg, where he occasionally built or rented a town house but usually stayed in one of the numerous taverns near the Capitol.

The life of this bygone century, even for white Virginians, was crude by modern standards. The death rate of children was appalling. The average

man had little education. Women had few legal rights. Boys were apprenticed to a trade at fourteen or younger. Indentured servants, who sold their services in exchange for passage from England, lived in bondage for about five to seven years. So did convict servants, whose sentences had been commuted to deportation.

Yet life in colonial Virginia had many rewards—again for whites. The advancing frontier offered opportunities. Even indentured servants could look forward to freedom and a future brighter than could usually be attained in England. It was an age of change and of promise, and the hand of authority did not bear too heavily. It was also a hospitable period, and there was always plenty to eat and drink.

Some of the pleasures but few of the promises of this life extended to black Virginians. Most were field hands on large plantations, upon which the colony's economy depended. In Williamsburg, an "urban center" for its time, the great majority of slaves performed domestic duties; a few became skilled craftsmen. The city Negro was probably better off than his plantation brother—better trained and more influenced by community life. But in town or country he was regarded as property first and only incidentally as a person. Propertyless and illiterate, he left few material vestiges or written records. The reality of his everyday life is therefore difficult for present-day historians to reconstruct in detail.

Williamsburg and Revolution

Restored Williamsburg recalls not only those years when it served as the seat of government for Britain's largest colony in America, but also the turbulent period when it was the political headquarters for Virginia patriots who had an important part in overthrowing the rule of the crown.

In the crucial decade before the Revolution, Williamsburg was a training and proving ground for leaders. Here George Washington, Thomas Jefferson, Patrick Henry, George Mason, Peyton Randolph, and Richard Henry Lee met and debated with other gifted contemporaries; their discussions and their written words did much to change the course of America. When the Declaration of Independence was proclaimed, a significant period of transition came to an end; the city had changed from the proud capital of a British colony to the even prouder capital of a new state in a new nation.

The Years Between

Williamsburg was the wartime capital of the young commonwealth from 1776 to 1780. Later, during the last decisive campaign of the war, it served briefly as headquarters first for Cornwallis, and after he had established his army at Yorktown, for Washington and Rochambeau. Although never a battlefield, the city did not escape the impact of war. Many of its men served the patriot cause, and the wounded from the siege lines of Yorktown were carried on wagons over twelve miles of muddy road to improvised hospitals at the Palace and the College.

After 1780, when the capital was moved to Richmond, Williamsburg stepped backstage in history, to resume its prominence only when the restoration project began in 1926. In the years between, however, the city occasionally saw exciting days as when, in 1824, Lafayette returned to be feted by the community. During the Civil War, Williamsburg's strategic position on the peninsula placed it between contending armies, and it became briefly the headquarters of Confederate General Joseph Johnston and then of Union General George McClellan. The battle of Williamsburg was fought in 1862 just east of town.

Throughout most of these years Williamsburg was a small college town and county seat. Its former importance lay buried in history and memory, as well as in the weathered colonial buildings that survived to stir the imagination of those who envisioned the city restored to its original beauty and dignity.

The Restoration of Williamsburg

The Reverend W. A. R. Goodwin, former rector of Bruton Parish Church, long cherished a dream of preserving the historic part of the old city of Williamsburg. He communicated this vision to Mr. John D. Rockefeller, Jr., who, taking the first step in 1926, determined to preserve the heart of this colonial capital, and, for more than thirty years, gave the project personal leadership. During his lifetime, Mr. Rockefeller not only contributed the funds necessary to accomplish the work of historical preservation and restoration and to develop facilities for the accommodation of the visiting public, but also set up an endowment to help provide for the permanence of the restoration and its educational programs.

Mr. Rockefeller's regard for Williamsburg arose, as did that of his friend Dr. Goodwin, not only from the visible remains of the former capital but also from its obvious value as a continuing symbol of pivotal years in our emergence as a nation. Mr. Rockefeller once expressed the deep meaning the project had for him in these words:

"The restoration of Williamsburg . . . offered an opportunity to restore a complete area and free it entirely from alien or inharmonious surroundings as well as to preserve the beauty and charm of the old buildings and gardens of the city and its historic significance. Thus it made a unique and irresistible appeal.

"As the work has progressed, I have come to feel that perhaps an even greater value is the lesson that it teaches of the patriotism, high purpose, and unselfish devotion of our forefathers to the common good."

The first major building to be restored was the Wren Building at the College of William and Mary, where initial work was completed in 1931. The College continues to use the building for classes and other purposes. Further restoration there in 1968 permitted it to become, through the cooperation of the College, a valuable adjunct to the interpretation of Williamsburg.

The Raleigh Tavern was opened to the public in 1932, followed by the Capitol (1934), Governor's Palace

(1934), Public Gaol (1936), George Wythe House (1940), and Brush-Everard House (1951). The Magazine, at one time exhibited by the Association for the Preservation of Virginia Antiquities, was leased and reopened as an exhibition building of Colonial Williamsburg in 1949. Wetherburn's Tavern, the Peyton Randolph House, and the James Geddy House and Shop were opened in 1968. Although it is an active Episcopal house of worship, Bruton Parish Church, restored in 1940, is made available for public visitation by its vestry. Of these buildings all but three (the Capitol, Palace, and Raleigh Tavern) are original eighteenth-century structures.

Carter's Grove, a prominent James River plantation in the eighteenth century, lies six miles southeast of Williamsburg. When its last private owner died in 1960, the Sealantic Fund, a Rockefeller family philanthropy, purchased the estate to insure its preservation and exhibition to the public. In 1969 Sealantic gave Carter's Grove to the Colonial Williamsburg Foundation. Careful study is now under way looking toward reestablishment of as much as possible of the plantation and domestic activity that would have gone on there two centuries ago. This will strengthen the interpretation of Williamsburg itself, for the colonial town was the political center of a great network of tidewater Virginia plantations.

Today the affairs of Colonial Williamsburg are conducted by *The Co-*

lonial *Williamsburg Foundation,* a not for profit educational organization deriving its financial support primarily from the public. The foundation's principal sources of income are admissions to the exhibition buildings, sales of authorized reproductions, books, and craft shop products, and revenues from hotel and restaurant accommodations provided for the convenience of the visiting public. The scope and diversity of the operations of Colonial Williamsburg are such that costs consistently exceed income. A portion of this deficit is offset by investment income from an en-

dowment fund provided by Mr. Rockefeller; however, Colonial Williamsburg depends primarily upon the support of the public, principally through the purchase of admissions, for the continuation of its historic preservation programs and educational activities.

"Restoration" and "Reconstruction"

This Guidebook makes frequent use of two terms—*restored* and *reconstructed. Restored* is applied to original buildings that were still standing in whole form or in signifi-

cant part and in most instances needed only to be repaired and stripped of later additions. *Reconstructed* is applied to structures that had fallen victim to fire or dismantling and had to be entirely rebuilt on their original sites. Eighty-eight buildings that survived from the eighteenth or early nineteenth century have been preserved or restored to their original appearance. More than half the major buildings, in fact, are original structures. Other important houses and their dependent outbuildings, such as smokehouses and kitchens, have been reconstructed. In both types of work, architects have been guided by archaeological remains, maps, drawings, photographs, insurance records, diaries, wills, and a vast range of other documentary materials and remaining physical evidence.

Outstanding documentary sources have included the "Frenchman's Map," drawn in 1782, probably for purposes of billeting Rochambeau's forces after the victory at Yorktown. A cherished possession of the Swem Library at the College of William and Mary, it has proved to be a reliable guide to the location, size, and shape of buildings throughout the Historic Area. The "Bodleian Plate," a copper engraving identified by Colonial Williamsburg historians in the Bodleian Library at Oxford, provided essential information about the architecture and landscaping of the Capitol, the Palace, and the Wren Building. A third document of great value has been Thomas Jefferson's own drawing of the floor plan of the Palace when he occupied it as governor; it is preserved at the Massachusetts Historical Society. These are unusual sources, however, and the restoration of Williamsburg has been made possible by thousands of small historical details uncovered by years of patient searching.

To complete the Historic Area, a few additional buildings are planned, either for exhibition or private use. The house of John Custis, father of Martha Washington's first husband, and the first public mental hospital will rise once more on France Street. Farther east the house of Robert Carter Nicholas—and later of President John Tyler—will take the place of a former city and county courthouse. Someday, too, the first theater

in English America may again face Palace Green.

The Modern City

During restoration work, modern conveniences and services were hidden rather than eliminated. Telephone and electric wires were placed underground and fire hydrants were made inconspicuous. Houses to be used for residential purposes have modern plumbing, insulation, and other features that would have startled the colonial owners. Occupants of some of the houses are Williamsburg residents who agreed to allow their homes to be restored in return for the right of lifetime occupancy. Many of the houses in the Historic Area not open as exhibition buildings are rented to Colonial Williamsburg employees, and the interiors are furnished according to the tenants' individual tastes, although the building exteriors and grounds are maintained by the foundation as part of the active museum scene.

Merchants Square, at the western end of Duke of Gloucester Street, is a business district with modern shops and visitor services. Although designed to harmonize with the town's colonial architecture, it was developed to meet modern community and visitor requirements. It should also be noted that the Historic Area, while conspicuous, constitutes only a portion of the present city.

Williamsburg today is administered by a mayor, council, and city manager. Close to 10,000 persons, including college students, live within the city limits, and many residents of nearby counties use Williamsburg as a business or marketing center. Three distinguished institutions founded in colonial days continue to take their place in the community—Bruton Parish (1674), the College of William and Mary (1693), and Eastern State Hospital (1773).

The College of William and Mary and Colonial Williamsburg jointly sponsor the Institute of Early American History and Culture (established in 1943) for research and publication. The institute publishes the *William and Mary Quarterly* and books by scholars throughout the United States, concentrating on the period from the discovery of America to about 1815.

Two other major American landmarks—Jamestown and Yorktown—lie close to Williamsburg. At Jamestown, ten miles southwest via the beautiful Colonial Parkway, one may see the site of the first permanent English settlement in the New World. Thirteen miles east of Williamsburg via the parkway is Yorktown, where Cornwallis surrendered to General Washington in 1781 after the last decisive battle of the Revolution. Within easy driving distance are Carter's Grove and several other historic James River plantations.

That the Future May Learn from the Past

In today's Williamsburg there is much to recall the color and drama of the colonial city and the everyday life of its citizens. But Williamsburg signifies more than physical restoration of buildings and gardens. It also reflects Mr. Rockefeller's conviction that the project has a vital purpose for present and future generations.

In accord with that conviction and as an ideal setting for the discussion of twentieth-century topics, Colonial Williamsburg sponsors a number of educational events, annual meetings, and seminars. Each element of this continuing educational program has a dominant purpose: to encourage both the casual visitor and the specialized participant to deepen his awareness and understanding of what has gone before.

THE INFORMATION CENTER

ALL VISITORS are invited and urged to go first to the Information Center, located on the fringe of the Historic Area (see map). This is the gateway to the colonial city of Williamsburg and the first step of a journey into the past.

Here the visitor may plan his stay, purchase tickets of admission, make reservations for lodging and dining, and board one of the buses that run continuously throughout the day to the Historic Area. Official publications, other books of historical interest, post cards, and color slides may be purchased here. He may also obtain information about nearby Carter's Grove plantation, Jamestown, Yorktown, and other historic sites and attractions in Virginia.

The Group Arrivals Building, located in the Information Center area, serves all adult and student group arrivals. Ticketing, orientation of groups, and special educational programs are conducted in this facility.

Adjacent are parking spaces for 2,900 cars. To avoid the inconvenience of traffic or parking problems in the restored city, visitors are encouraged to leave their cars at the Information Center and make use of the buses, which may be boarded at the lower level of the building.

The Motor House, Cafeteria, and Cascades Restaurant

These modern buildings form a concentration of visitor facilities for Colonial Williamsburg adjacent to the Information Center. All are owned and operated by the Colonial Williamsburg Foundation. The Motor House offers more than 300 guest rooms, a central lounge, and swimming pools. The 600-seat Cafeteria serves a wide choice of dishes throughout the day, while the Self-Service Grill offers quick service of popular foods. The Cascades Restaurant provides a fine cuisine of regional and international dishes, and has a number of separate dining and meeting rooms.

THE CAPITOL

AT THE eastern end of Duke of Gloucester Street stands the reconstructed Capitol, one of the chief exhibition buildings of Colonial Williamsburg. For the better part of a century—from 1704 to 1780—Virginia's General Assembly convened on this historic site. Here an embarrassed and stammering Washington was applauded by fellow burgesses for his part in the French and Indian War; here Patrick Henry defiantly protested the Stamp Act until accused of treason; here George Mason's Virginia Declaration of Rights was passed. In this building the House of Burgesses, America's oldest representative assembly, held its meetings, as did the smaller, more aristocratic Council. The General Court sat in the paneled courtroom to try all the important Virginia cases, civil and criminal.

When the governor rode in his coach from the Palace to open the Assembly, he symbolized the power of the English king from the sea to the unexplored frontier of the huge wilderness empire then claimed by Virginia. Laws enacted in the Capitol affected the whole colony, and legislators who met here included virtually every Virginian of note in the eighteenth century. The Capitol was the scene of stubborn opposition to what the colonists re-

garded as arbitrary policies of the king and Parliament; here, claiming the rights and privileges of British subjects, Virginians sought to defend their concept of self-government—a concept that had taken root when the burgesses first met in Jamestown in 1619 and that had matured through the years. In the end the lawmakers reluctantly took up arms against the mother country; yet their prolonged effort to achieve their goal by peaceful means is a conspicuous testament to their respect for the processes of deliberation carried on within the walls of the Capitol.

In the troubled spring of 1776 occurred the most stirring historical events associated with the Capitol. It was on May 15 of that year that Virginia's legislators here pledged their lives and fortunes on the daring hazard of full freedom from England. Although the colonies were weak and divided, and were defying one of the greatest military powers of the

day, these men in Williamsburg had the spirit and vision to adopt a Resolution for American Independence without a dissenting voice. On June 7, Virginia's delegate, Richard Henry Lee, acted on these instructions and introduced a motion to its effect on the floor of the Continental Congress at Philadelphia. This led directly to the Declaration of Independence, drafted largely by Thomas Jefferson, who had once stood at the half-open door of the House of Burgesses to hear Patrick Henry thunder his defiance of Parliament and king.

Each year the period from May 15 through July 4 is celebrated as the "Prelude to Independence." On the anniversary of the independence resolution in 1953, President Eisenhower, standing just in front of the original speaker's chair in the House of Burgesses, said, "I think no American could stand in these halls and on this spot without feeling a very great and deep sense of the debt we owe to the courage, the stamina, and faith of our forefathers."

When the legislature was in session or the court convened, the public grounds bordering the Capitol teemed with Virginians of every rank and profession. The broad, grassy "street" to the east of the Capitol was called the "Exchange," where men met in the open air to transact their commercial and financial business. Within a stone's throw were at least a dozen inns, taverns, ordinaries, and coffeehouses, serving everything from Virginia ham and local beer to Barbados sweetmeats and French brandy. Nearby stood the city's second theater, where Shakespeare's *Merchant of Venice* was the opening play. Stables were to be found convenient to the square. A line of paper mulberry trees edges the square, their gnarled and herniated trunks exciting comment.

Capitol Square was a natural center for celebrations. In 1746 word reached Williamsburg that the duke of Cumberland had finally routed Bonnie Prince Charlie and his dispirited Highlanders. That night there was a gala ball at the Capitol, where three tables were piled high with "near 100 dishes after the most delicate taste." Outside, after each of the twenty toasts, volleys were discharged from cannon lined up on the green.

The Capitol was ordered built by an act of 1699, less than one year after the last of several statehouses in Jamestown had succumbed to fire. As a drastic precaution against this danger, Williamsburg's first Capitol was designed without chimneys, and the use of fire, candles, or tobacco was strictly prohibited. In time such safeguards were sacrificed to necessity and convenience; a secretary complained, for example, that his records were "exposed by the Damps." In 1723 two chimneys were added. Candles were brought in, and doubtless permission was soon granted to smoke tobacco—Virginia's "bewitching vegetable." Whether from these sources, or from arson (as was supposed at the time), the building was gutted

by fire on January 30, 1747, "and the naked Brick Walls only left standing."

With the encouragement of Governor William Gooch, the "Royal Fabric" was ordered rebuilt. This second Capitol, completed in 1753, incorporated the surviving walls of its predecessor but differed in appearance. After the removal of Virginia's government to Richmond in 1780, the second building fell into disrepair, and in 1832 it too was destroyed by fire.

Before reconstruction could be undertaken, Colonial Williamsburg faced a dilemma: should the first or second building rise again on the old foundations? The second Capitol was of greater historic interest since it witnessed the events of the years before the Revolution, but the first Capitol could lay claim to greater architectural distinction, its rounded ends, for instance, being unique. Long searching of the architectural evidence disclosed voluminous information about the earlier building, whereas few records were available for the later. It is the first Capitol that is here reconstructed.

The foundations for the original building were laid in 1701. During its construction under the supervision of "master builder" Henry Cary, Virginia's lawmakers met in the Wren Building of the College but moved impatiently into the new Capitol in 1704, a year before its final completion was symbolized by the surrender of the builder's keys to the speaker of the House of Burgesses.

The period of the Capitol is signified by the coat of arms of Queen Anne emblazoned on its tower, and by the flag of the Great Union (the eighteenth-century form of the British Union Jack) which usually flies overhead. The style of architecture, with round and arched windows and a cupola, is of the Renaissance, but simplification was imposed by conditions in a young colony, as evidenced by the absence of colonades or an elaborate facade.

The H-shaped plan is an early example of an architectural design successfully devised for a specific purpose. It also reflects the makeup of Virginia's colonial government. One wing contains the Hall of the House of Burgesses (on the first floor) and committee rooms for the burgesses (on the second). The other wing,

finished and furnished much more elaborately, houses the General Courtroom (on the first floor), and the Council Chamber (on the second). Each wing has its own staircase. On the second floor—appropriately linking the two wings—is the Conference Room, where burgesses and councillors met together for morning prayer or held joint conferences to resolve disagreements. The composition of

the building is set off by the tall hexagonal cupola and is skillfully defined on Capitol Square by a sturdy brick wall.

The site and the original foundations of the Capitol were faithfully preserved over the years by the Association for the Preservation of Virginia Antiquities, and were generously deeded by that organization to Colonial Williamsburg. The rebuilt Capitol was opened in 1934 by the House of Delegates and the Senate of the Commonwealth of Virginia, meeting in joint session. At this time a bill was passed enabling the General Assembly to convene in the colonial Capitol at times that might seem proper, a practice that in peacetime has been followed on some occasion during alternate sessions. At the dedication in 1934 the Assembly was addressed by Governor George C. Peery, and by Mr. John D. Rockefeller, Jr., whose discourse included the words: "What a temptation to sit in silence and let the past speak to us of those great patriots whose voices once resounded in these halls, and whose farseeing wisdom, high courage, and unselfish devotion to the common good will ever be an inspiration to noble living."

Public Records Office—N.

After the Capitol was gutted by fire in 1747, the Council decided to provide for "the Preservation of the Public Records and Papers" in a separate building—an example followed

Palmer House—S.

John Palmer's long residence on this site was rudely interrupted on an April evening in 1754 by a devastating fire. It started, according to one report, through the neglect of the keeper of a neighboring store "in leaving a fire too carelessly . . . while he staid longer than he intended at a Public House." The writer expressed the opinion that "with any tolerable management, the fire might easily been extinguished," but word that a quantity of gunpowder was in the building "struck a general terror for a considerable time." Eventually "the Powder Catched."

Palmer, a distinguished lawyer and bursar of the College, had come into possession of the property sometime before 1749 and occupied it until his death in 1760. The present house,

in other colonies. Accordingly, this one-story building, without basement, was constructed with a view to safety. The sloping chimney caps, designed to prevent downdrafts in the flues, the plastered window jambs, the interior partitions of brick, and the masonry floor all reflect the builders' fear of fire.

The hip roof is characteristic of public buildings in the eighteenth century. A fine pedimented doorway in rubbed brick adds dignity to the facade. The rounded front steps, similar in design to others in Williamsburg, are of blue Shrewsbury stone. The building served as the office of the secretary of the colony until the capital was moved to Richmond in 1780. The court of admiralty and the city of Williamsburg used it for a time, and the building later became an adjunct of the Williamsburg Grammar School, which was opened in 1784 in the old Capitol.

The Public Records Office periodically houses temporary exhibits that relate to the educational programs of Colonial Williamsburg, at which times it is open to visitors.

now restored, was presumably built by him to replace the one lost in the fire. In rebuilding he may have used brick from the earlier house, built by Alexander Kerr, a Scottish jeweler and merchant, who had died in 1738. Construction was evidently in progress in 1736 when the burgesses made complaint against Kerr for "several encroachments . . . particularly in setting a Brick-Kiln upon the Capitol Bounds." It was customary in colonial days for bricks to be made of clay dug from the cellar and fired on the spot in an improvised kiln. The "put-log" holes in the brickwork were left by the masons who built the house when they removed their scaffolding.

During the Civil War the house served as military headquarters first for Confederate General Joseph Johnston and then for Union General George McClellan. The garden is open to the public; the house is privately occupied.

Marot's Ordinary—S.

In colonial Virginia an "ordinary" was the same as an inn or tavern.

John (or Jean) Marot, a Huguenot refugee, started his career in Virginia about 1700, when William Byrd I of Westover employed him as a servant; he had become a substantial property holder seventeen years later when he met a violent death, allegedly murdered by a fellow ordinary-keeper, Francis Sharp. Marot was William Byrd I's "man"—perhaps secretary—until Byrd's death in 1704. Moving to Williamsburg, he bought this property in 1708 and operated an ordinary patronized by the gentry. Although for several years a constable of the city, Marot twice ran afoul of the law for "Selling Liquors at Higher Rates" than set by the York County Court. In both cases he pleaded guilty, submitted to the judgment of the court, and was excused.

Marot's widow continued the ordinary until 1738 when she leased it to John Taylor. By 1745 it had been taken over by the Marots' daughter Anne and her husband, James Shields; they apparently named it the English Coffee House. In 1751, after Shields's death, Daniel Fisher leased the place and rented apartments, one of his tenants being the celebrated character actor Lewis Hallam, whose "Company of Comedians" was playing at the new theater on Waller Street in 1752. Dr. John de Sequeyra, the first visiting physician to the Public Hospital, leased the eastern end of the house in 1772 and occupied it for a number of years thereafter. Privately occupied.

Burdett's Ordinary—N.

A swinging sign of Edinburgh Castle hangs where John Burdett once kept his ordinary. It was a typical, run-of-the-mill tavern, used chiefly for drinking and gambling, although meals were also served. During Publick Times the ten beds owned by Burdett were probably fully occupied. At Burdett's death, his inventory included the characteristic effects of his trade: numerous pewter and delftware plates, "1 old Fiddle," "1 Billiard Table with sticks, Balls, etc." "11 pr. Dice," and "a Quantity of choice old *Madeira* Wine, and old *Barbados* Rum."

A sketch clearly showing the unusual projecting porch chamber was drawn in 1743 as evidence in a lawsuit concerning the property line between the ordinary and the house next door to the west. The survival of this document made accurate reconstruction possible. Privately occupied.

John Crump House—N.

In 1717 the trustees of Williamsburg granted this lot to Francis

Sharp. Sharp apparently complied promptly with a building clause, then customary, requiring that a building be erected within twenty-four months, for the following year he obtained a license to offer "good wholesome and cleanly lodging and diet for Travellers."

The early house is shown on the sketch mentioned in connection with Burdett's Ordinary next door. The house was built in stages during the eighteenth century and as many as three tenants are known to have occupied it at one time. The building was purchased in 1789 by John Crump, then jailor of the city of

Williamsburg. His son, also named John, operated an ordinary here during the first decade of the nineteenth century. Reconstructed; privately occupied.

Nicolson Shop—N.

This distinctive red building is representative of the two-story frame shops that were common in eighteenth-century Williamsburg. As in other examples, the second floor was used for residence or storage. Robert

Nicolson acquired the property in 1773 and had both a tailor shop and store here. The lot was owned earlier by William Wharton and, from 1717, by John Marot and his heirs.

The dismantling of a large nineteenth-century building exposed the original framework of the shop, now restored. A structure of little architectural pretension, it reflects the openly commercial purpose for which it was erected. Privately occupied.

Pasteur-Galt Apothecary Shop—N.

The mortar and pestle of the gaily painted sign, and the snake-entwined staff that can be seen on the mortar itself, identify this as the shop of an apothecary and doctor. It is one of Colonial Williamsburg's operating craft shops, exhibiting an imposing array of the elixirs and ointments of colonial medicine and "compleat Setts of amputating Instruments."

Delftware jars of medicinal herbs and aromatic spices line the proprietor's shelves. Tobacco and other wares are carried as valuable sidelines just as they were in colonial days.

Most eighteenth-century apothecaries were also doctors; not only did they prescribe and dispense medicines, they also knew how to use surgical tools. Dr. William Pasteur had an apothecary shop here in 1760. Fifteen years later he took into partnership a promising young surgeon, John Minson Galt, former undergraduate at the College of William and Mary, who had received his medical training in London. The room at the rear of the shop has been furnished as the office of the two doctors. Later Galt won honors as a field surgeon during the Revolution. His desk, chair, and surgical instruments—loaned by his descendants—are on display in the shop.

The simulated stone facing on the front of the reconstructed building, known as rustication, was an arti-

ficiality that appealed to some in colonial times when building stone was difficult and expensive to obtain. Behind the shop is an herb garden open to the public.

Scrivener House—N.

Although one of Williamsburg's smaller buildings, this house characteristically retains the same scale as its larger neighbors in cornice, window, door, chimney, and other details. This creates what one architect describes as "a happy feeling of pre-

John Coke Office—S.

John Coke, the grandson of goldsmith and tavern-keeper John Coke, operated the Raleigh Tavern for a short time in the early 1800s but little is known of how he used the building now reconstructed on this site. Privately occupied.

Alexander Craig House—N.

In 1771 a saddler named Alexander Craig, who had operated his saddle and harness shop on a part of the lot since 1755, purchased this frame residence. Earlier owners included an innkeeper, a glazier, and a perukemaker. Like many other Williams-

tension" for the householder of modest means. The building has been reconstructed from a photograph taken before the house was destroyed. From 1762 until 1772 a store was conducted here by Joseph Scrivener, whose diversified inventory included West India goods (rum, sugar, molasses, coffee, and ginger), East India Company wares (tea, pepper, and allspice), and Spanish and Portuguese commodities (wine, vinegar, and salt). The personal effects listed in the inventory were largely of British manufacture. Privately occupied.

burg dwellings, the house grew in stages, but without losing its early individuality. Additions were made during the 1700s, the latest being the long shed roof at the rear. The space between the chimneys at the western end of the house was enclosed to provide closets. A geomatic garden with boxwood topiary fronts on the street, affording a view of the outbuildings. The kitchen garden is beyond. Original brick is incorporated in the walks. Restored; privately occupied.

Alexander Purdie House—S.

In 1767 this property was bought by Alexander Purdie, printer and at that time coeditor, with John Dixon, of the *Virginia Gazette.* He later established his own newspaper and printing office at Tarpley's Store nearby. Purdie not only lived in the house, but his first wife operated a store here, selling millinery, jewelry, men's stockings, etc. Near the end of the century the house was briefly occupied by Cyrus Griffin, in 1788

president of Congress under the Articles of Confederation.

Rebuilt on the exact lines of the old foundation, it is now connected by a concealed passageway to the King's Arms Tavern next door, and forms part of the restaurant operated there. The outbuildings are grouped around a paved court that adjoins a formal garden open to the public. Beyond are a paddock and stable that front on Francis Street.

King's Arms Tavern—S.

Now a public restaurant operated by the Colonial Williamsburg Foundation, this reconstructed inn again caters to the appetite as well as the eye. Jane Vobe operated here one of the most genteel taverns in the city, with a clientele that included William Byrd III, Sir Peyton Skipwith, and George Washington. Today, paneling and handsome furnishings of eighteenth-century design lend an air of hospitality and comfort. A wine vault rivals its colonial predecessor. The gambrel roof is given an interesting texture by the shingles with round butts, which were commonly used in Williamsburg. (Their purpose, however, was utilitarian rather than decorative. Square-ended shingles tend to warp and curl when dried out quickly in the hot Virginia sun.)

At the rear of the tavern is the garden, in which meals are also served, weather permitting. The

King's Arms specializes in traditional southern dishes: Virginia ham, fried chicken, scalloped oysters, roast beef, Sally Lunn bread. Many dishes, based on recipes of colonial days, are delectable enough to dispose of the complaint of one eighteenth-century gourmet that "Heaven sends good Meat, But the Devil sends Cooks!"

Appetites were prodigious in that bygone century, and it was not unusual for the menu to include two "main courses," each consisting of perhaps a dozen dishes. Wine, or a tankard of beer, rounded out the repast.

The King's Arms, although outranked in historical fame by the Raleigh Tavern, has many associations with the past In 1778 the Ohio Company of Virginia, then pressing its great land claims in the west, met here. During the Revolution, when Mrs. Vobe supplied food and drink to American troops, the energetic

Baron Steuben ran up a bill of nearly three hundred dollars for lodging, meals, and drinks for himself and his servants, and entertainment for his guests. After the Revolution the King's Arms was renamed Eagle Tavern.

King's Arms Barber Shop—S.

Here, in another of Colonial Williamsburg's operating craft shops, a perukemaker patiently awaits the vanished trade of two centuries ago. Basin, razor, and soap dish rest beside a chromeless colonial barber chair. Close by is the cone-shaped mask that a gentleman clapped firmly over his face to allow him to breathe while the barber powdered his hair. A lady's wig, or hair, was dressed at home. Materials are at hand to fashion wigs of every description, and there are tools to curl and care for them. Reconstructed.

RALEIGH TAVERN

Situated on the north side of Duke of Gloucester Street at the center of the busiest block in Williamsburg, the many-dormered Raleigh stood firmly in the foreground of life in the colonial capital. Most famous of Williamsburg hostelries, it was appropriately dedicated to Sir Walter Raleigh, who took a leading part in sending colonists to the New World and in encouraging the use of tobacco in England. A leaden bust of Sir Walter adorns the main doorway. The reconstructed tavern is one of the two taverns now included among the exhibition buildings of Colonial Williamsburg.

During all the year, but most particularly at Publick Times, the Raleigh was a center of social activity. Balls held in its Apollo Room were second in elegance only to those in the Governor's Palace itself. Planters and merchants gathered at its bar. Sturdy tavern tables were scarred by diceboxes. Tobacco smoke from long clay pipes filled the air, together with heated political discussions. Good fellowship was sealed by a toast of Madeira or hot rum punch, or by a pint of ale drunk from a pewter tankard.

George Washington, although he generally stopped elsewhere, often noted in his dairy that he "dined at the Raleigh." After one evening of revelry in the year 1763, Thomas Jefferson, then reading law under the learned George Wythe's supervision, complained in a letter to John Page: "Last night, as merry as agreeable company and dancing with *Belinda* in the *Apollo* could make me, I never could have thought the succeeding Sun would have seen me so wretched."

Public receptions were common. In 1775 the Williamsburg Volunteers met here in honor of Peyton Randolph's return from Philadelphia, where he had served as first president of the Continental Congress. The following year, when Virginia troops in Williamsburg heard that their esteemed commander, Patrick Henry, was about to leave them, the officers gave a dinner here in his honor. When the Treaty of Paris ending the Revolution was proclaimed in the city, the citizens of the new republic appropriately concluded their triumphal parade by a celebration at their principal tavern. Lafayette was welcomed on his return to Williamsburg in 1824 by a banquet in the Apollo attended by the governor and Council and by many notables including John Marshall and John C. Calhoun. Perhaps the last great reception held in the old Raleigh was in 1859, when the "fair and accomplished ladies of Williamsburg" arranged a banquet for alumni of the College—including former President Tyler. In December of that year the hostelry was leveled by fire.

The Raleigh was a center of business activity and the scene of many public auctions. Land, slaves, and goods were bought and sold "before the door of the Raleigh," and the tavern ranked with the Printing Office as a postal and news center: mail to go by sea was dispatched here, and newly arrived guests often served as the most effective "newspapers" of the day.

The aroused colonists met at the Raleigh to discuss grievances against the arbitrary policies of king and Parliament. When Governor Botetourt dissolved the Assembly in 1769 because of its protest against the British Revenue Act, many indignant burgesses reconvened at the tavern to draw up a boycott of British goods. Five years later, other nonimportation measures were agreed upon at the Raleigh after the shocking news reached Virginia that Britain had ordered the port of Boston closed.

Additional important meetings at the Raleigh foreshadowed American independence. In 1773 five patriots, Thomas Jefferson, his brother-in-law Dabney Carr, Patrick Henry, and the brothers Richard Henry and Francis Lightfoot Lee, gathered in a private room here to weigh the need for closer cooperation among all the colonies in the growing dispute with England. "Not thinking our old and leading members up to the point of forwardness and zeal which the time required," as Jefferson wrote, these burgesses took the lead in organizing Virginia's Committee of Correspondence. The following year, the Assembly being again dissolved, the "representatives of the people" met here to issue the call for the first Continental Congress.

Architects who reconstructed the tavern were aided by two wood engravings made by Benson J. Lossing in 1848, by insurance policies, and by archaeological excavation that revealed most of the original foundations of the building and many colonial artifacts. The furnishing of the Raleigh was guided by the painstaking inventories of early proprietors. After the death of Anthony Hay in 1770, every article in the tavern was listed. The gentlemen of colonial Virginia and their ladies would find little change if they returned to dance again their minuets, and charter members of the Phi Beta Kappa Society, founded in Williamsburg in 1776, could again meet in the Apollo Room. The Raleigh's pervasive spirit of hospitality is well expressed in the motto gilded over the Apollo Room mantel: *Hilaritas Sapientiae et Bonae Vitae Proles*—"Jollity, the offspring of wisdom and good living."

Raleigh Tavern Bakery—N.

In this operating craft shop breads and cakes are mixed and baked from recipes, ingredients, and equipment common two hundred years ago. The baker in colonial garb performs every step of the baking process by hand, using two red brick dome-shaped ovens rebuilt from documents, drawings, and actual remains. The bakery occupies part of the reconstructed Raleigh Tavern Kitchen.

The Unicorn's Horn and John Carter's Store—N.

The handsome and substantial brick building originally at this site

was erected in 1765 by two brothers, John and Dr. James Carter. John Carter operated a general store in the east portion of the building, in 1767 advertising a potpourri of wares including "ounce threads, shoe soles, Lilly's grammars, ink powder and sand boxes, saucepans, castle soap and rhenish wine," all to be sold "for ready money only." John's brother, Dr. James Carter, ran an apothecary shop in the west portion under the distinctive sign of the unicorn's horn. He advertised in the same year a large assortment of imported drugs and medicines, including "Spanish licorice," "Ladies sticking plaister, Greenhow's tincture for the teeth," and "Mrs. Rednap's red fit drops." A third brother, Dr. William Carter, later joined Dr. James Carter at the apothecary shop and in 1779 took over the business. The building, which occupied a choice commercial location next door to the Raleigh Tavern, was destroyed by the same fire that consumed the Raleigh in 1859. Now reconstructed, both parts are privately occupied.

Charlton House—S.

This is a typical two-story Williamsburg house, with a central entrance and a chimney at each end. The simplicity of the design is relieved by the enrichment of detail in the cornices and windowsill moldings.

The house was associated with the Charltons, Edward and Richard. Richard, a tavern-keeper, frequently played host to George Washington.

Edward, a wigmaker, occupied a shop in an excellent location next to the Raleigh Tavern. An account book that came to light in a Williamsburg attic gives a valuable picture of his barbering activities and shows that among his clientele were Thomas Jefferson, Patrick Henry, George Wythe, Peyton Randolph, and many others whose names appear in this Guidebook. Charges for wigmaking, shaving, and hairdressing for many of these gentlemen were carried on a yearly basis. The brown dress bob wigs then in fashion cost them 43 shillings. About 1762, Edward married Jane Hunter, milliner and shopkeeper. Like many Williamsburg craftsmen, he served on the city's common council. The house is restored; privately occupied.

The Golden Ball—N.

James Craig, a jeweler who bought this shop in 1765 and employed a clockmaker, once set a pair of earrings for Patsy Custis, the beloved but ill-fated stepdaughter of George Washington. Jewelers and silversmiths

ranked high among craftsmen and were respected members of the community. For example, Anthony Singleton, who was once apprenticed to Craig, married Governor Benjamin Harrison's daughter.

One of the most common rings supplied by jewelers of the period was the mourning ring, often given by the surviving husband or wife to friends as well as to members of the family. Examples of such rings may be seen today in the Golden Ball, one of the craft shops operated by Colonial Williamsburg. Here a jeweler and engraver again practice their exacting crafts as they did two centuries ago.

Visitors to the Golden Ball will see a collection of mid-eighteenth-century clocks, examples of fine cutlery, and jewelry. A silver tobacco box, made by Edward Cornock in 1723, was given to Colonial Williamsburg in 1954 by the Queen Mother of England and is now in the shop.

The original house on this site, probably erected before 1724, survived until 1907 when it was torn down. Photographs and the recol-lections of residents made the reconstruction possible.

Margaret Hunter Shop—N.

Here milady of the twentieth century may step into a shop that was once a favorite of planters' wives. Once again the milliner fashions and decorates hats of Tuscan and Leghorn straw. Again counters are filled with soap, buttons, fans, knitting needles, breast flowers, and with such substantial and eye-filling fabrics as were once imported from England. This too is one of the operating craft shops of the Historic Area.

Trained in England, Margaret Hunter came over to join her sister Jane in the millinery business, which she carried on alone when Jane married Edward Charlton, the wigmaker. Shortly after 1770 Margaret opened a shop in this building. Her advertisements in the *Virginia Gazette* show the varied nature of the milliner's

calling in the eighteenth century. They list jet necklaces and earrings, "black love ribands," "Sleeve Knots," "Stuff Shoes for Ladies," women's and children's riding habits, toys, Scotch snuff, and busts of the late governor, the popular Lord Botetourt. In addition to ladies' hats and bonnets, milliners offered to make "Cloaks and Cardinals," dresses, and sometimes "Gentlemens Linen."

Cardinals are the short, hooded capes, originally made of scarlet cloth, which are now worn by hostesses in Williamsburg on chilly days. The hostess gowns are adapted from those worn during the third quarter of the eighteenth century, a period when ladies affected neither wigs nor powdered hair.

Buildings belonging to the merchant firm of Harmer and King were standing on this site by 1745. The small brick storehouse that survived has been restored to its early appearance. Like many other buildings planned for commercial use, the gable end is toward the street. The brickwork is original except for necessary patching.

Russell House—N.

After occupancy by a merchant, apothecary, and milliner, the house

on this site became in 1774 the home of one William Russell. It resembles many other small Williamsburg houses, but eighteenth-century builders varied the use of individual elements of design in ways that lend character to the street scene as a whole. Here the treatment of the entrance to one side does not destroy the essential symmetry. Reconstructed; privately occupied.

WETHERBURN'S TAVERN

HENRY WETHERBURN bought this property in 1738, shortly thereafter built the eastern portion of the present structure, and ten years later added the western portion. The building has been in continuous use for more than two hundred years as, at different times, a home, tavern, store, boarding house, girls' school, guest house, and shop. The property is now leased for exhibition by Colonial Williamsburg from the Bucktrout-Braithwaite Foundation.

Wetherburn was already well known as a tavern-keeper in Williamsburg during the previous seven years. His career was well launched when he married the widow of an innkeeper, Henry Bowcock, and thereby became executor of the bride's late husband's estate. It was shortly after this that one of his customers, Wil-

liam Randolph, prescribed "Henry Wetherburn's biggest Bowl of Arrack Punch" to seal the transaction when he deeded two hundred acres of land to Peter Jefferson, father-to-be of Thomas.

Wetherburn was probably Williamsburg's most successful eighteenth-century innkeeper, at times having an interest in several taverns at once. He was host at the Raleigh, for instance, for a period after he purchased this property. Another boost to his career came in 1751, when his wife died. On the day she was buried a town diarist recorded that "he has found her hoard, they say." A week later Wetherburn married Mrs. Anne Marot Ingles Shields, the widow of another innkeeper (and also the daughter of an earlier one). Again he assumed the executorship of an estate that included tavern property and furnishings.

After his death in 1760 his heirs leased the tavern to other innkeepers, notably James Southall and Robert Anderson. The inventory of Wetherburn's estate, a long and detailed one, listed the contents of the building room by room. It has been a principal guide in furnishing the restored building.

Additional information came from the painstaking excavations made by Colonial Williamsburg archaeologists. They recovered more than 192,000 artifacts from the soil of this site, including pieces of glass, porcelain, pottery, clay tobacco pipes, and a harvest of forty-two unbroken wine bottles that at one time in the eighteenth century seem to have contained brandied cherries.

Flooring throughout the building is for the most part original, with patching where necessary; plaster, on the other hand, is almost entirely new. Except where nineteenth-century alterations had removed interior walls, the framing is original, with some concealed reinforcement. Windows, trim, and weatherboarding are partly old, partly new. All outbuildings except the dairy, which is original, are reconstructions.

Like the Raleigh, Wetherburn's Tavern filled to overflowing twice a year at Publick Times, and at all times it stood near the center of commercial, social, and political activity in the colonial capital. It was the scene of auctions, balls, business conferences, and political meetings. The mayor and aldermen of Williamsburg gave a dinner at Wetherburn's in 1751 for the newly appointed Governor Dinwiddie and members of the Council. Washington frequently dined, supped, or spent the evening at this tavern during the years when it was run by Southall and Anderson.

According to the Wetherburn estate inventory there were fourteen beds in the various rooms on the second floor, and on the first floor "Mr. Pages Room" contained three and "the Chamber" two. Wetherburn thus could have slept as many as thirty-eight persons at once— counting two per bed. Of course all patrons were male. Women rarely stayed at colonial taverns because privacy was not to be found there. Instead, they put up in the homes of hospitable friends. However, ladies might well have patronized the tavern dining room along with their husbands.

The work of the tavern was done largely by slaves who had gained skill in cooking, cleaning, washing, serving, gardening, and stable tending. They were not tipped for their services—unless they performed some very special favor. At Wetherburn's death twelve slaves were listed at his tavern—four men, seven women, and a girl.

Tavern-keepers in colonial Virginia were subject to careful regulation by the county courts, beginning with the issuance of the required license to operate. The justices could restrict the number of licenses as a regulatory measure, or could refuse a license to someone they deemed unfit or who could not post the large bond called for. Other regulations set maximum prices that could be charged for lodging, food, liquor, and fodder; required the innkeeper to post his schedule of prices prominently in a public room; limited the amount of credit a tavern-keeper could extend; and condemned drunkenness and unlawful gambling.

Behind Wetherburn's is a practical garden for a working tavern.

Tarpley's Store—S.

This reconstructed building now houses a retail outlet where souvenir articles and craft shops products may be purchased. It is named for James Tarpley, merchant, who in 1761 presented to Bruton Parish Church the bell it has used ever since. In 1775 Alexander Purdie acquired the property, which he used, until his death in 1779, as headquarters for his new *Virginia Gazette*—a rival to that published by Dixon and Hunter. For a short time before the Revolution there were three different papers of the same name issued in Williamsburg, all weeklies. Purdie took as his

motto "Always for Liberty and the Public Good." Purdie was appointed public printer for Virginia in 1775, and later became the postmaster in Williamsburg by congressional appointment. At his printing shop he also sold books, stationery, and music for the harpsichord and violin.

Prentis House—N.

Archaeological excavations were particularly helpful in recreating this house. The foundations were unusually well preserved and the positions of brick walls and fence posts were clearly indicated. From this evidence it was possible to establish the location of the front fence that extends beyond the building line. From Botetourt

Street there is a good view of the outbuildings—the flanking storehouse and kitchen, the dairy, smokehouse, and wellhead around a paved yard, with a stable beyond the orchard. Mary Brooke, wife of a prosperous merchant, William Prentis, inherited the property from her father, John Brooke, who had built a house on the site between 1712 and 1714. The gardening diary and planting lists of a member of the family who had grown up here were used in designing the present neatly fenced gardens, which are open to the public. The reconstructed house is privately occupied.

INTERSECTION OF
BOTETOURT STREET

Davidson Shop—N.

This was once the apothecary shop of Robert Davidson, a "Practitioner in Physick" and mayor of Williamsburg in 1738, who supplied his clients with "Balsams, Decoctions, Electuaries, Elixirs, Emplaisters, Extracts, Infusions, Liquors, Magisteries, Oils, Ointments," and other remedies believed to soothe their ailments. The building, reconstructed, varies from the usual shop form in which the gable end faces the street. It provides wide display windows of an early type that are protected by a deep cornice, and a raised platform in front—a refuge from the inevitable mud or dust of unpaved streets in colonial days. The earliest owner of the property was Henry Gill, who built on

this and the neighboring lot soon after 1707 and for several years operated an ordinary here. Privately occupied.

Waters-Coleman House—N.

Most eighteenth-century housewives had little closet space, but the mistress of this house was more fortunate. At each end of the two-story frame dwelling, a roomy closet was made possible in the space formed between the pair of chimneys. Note also the repeat of the full cornice at the break in the steep gambrel roof; this provides cover for the jutting dormer windows. The reconstructed

house is named for two of its most prominent occupants: William Waters, who owned several plantations and bought it for his house in town, and William Coleman, a post-Revolutionary mayor of Williamsburg. Privately occupied.

Brick House Tavern—S.

Dr. William Carter, a leading businessman as well as surgeon and apothecary, acquired this property in 1761. He divided the building, selling part of it and renting the remainder. The multiple use is reflected in the six entrances. One proprietress advertised "12 or 14 very good lodging rooms, with fire places to most of them." Gentlemen slept on the upper floor, ladies on the first floor. The corner room provided a choice location for a shopkeeper. At one time Margaret Hunter had her millinery business here.

Accurate reconstruction of the building was possible because a detailed plan, drawn to scale, survived; also, the original foundations were unusually complete. The brickwork of the tavern is worthy of note. Like all bricks used in the restored or recon-

structed buildings, these were molded by hand in wooden molds and fired as in colonial days. In firing the local clay, it was found that the use of hardwood as fuel for the kiln produced the blue gray, glazed "headers" characteristic of old Williamsburg brick. The small wooden building behind is a reconstruction of a shop occupied in 1766 by a riding-chair maker. The tavern is, appropriately, operated today as a lodging facility of Williamsburg Inn.

James Anderson House—S.

Between 1755 and 1760 an original house on this lot was owned by William Withers, secretary to Governor Dinwiddie. Thereafter it was for some years operated as a tavern by Mrs. Christiana Campbell. It was here that George Washington frequently put up when he came to Williamsburg to attend the sessions as a member of the House of Burgesses. In 1770 blacksmith James Anderson purchased the property and later set up his forges to the rear of a newly built house. Before and during the Revolution Anderson served as public armorer of Virginia. His daughter Nancy Camp inherited the house, and a description

of it in an insurance policy taken out in her name aided the architects in the reconstruction. The Anderson House is open to the public and contains an extensive exhibit devoted to all phases of Williamsburg's archaeology.

Waters Storehouse—N.

Standing on part of the property owned by William Waters, the original of this building was probably erected by him to replace the storehouse he sold to William Holt in 1760. Waters died in 1767. Part of the livelihood of his widow, Sarah, then came from renting this storehouse and the shop on the corner (Davidson Shop). Like many others on Duke of Gloucester Street, these merchants found shopkeeping in Williamsburg precarious. Trade flourished during Publick Times, but competition was keen, the supply of goods uncertain, and most sales had

to be made on credit. The shop was reconstructed with the aid of drawings on insurance policies, and foundations revealed by excavation. Privately occupied.

Holt's Storehouse—N.

John Holt built a "new Store" here about 1745, stocking all kinds of merchandise: dry goods, haberdashery, china, and groceries. The sign of the three sugar loaves hanging above the entrance is the traditional insignia of grocers. John Holt was forced to sell the property in 1754. Six years later his brother William bought from the new owner, William Waters, part of the lot, with the "Storehouse thereon lately Erected," and kept a general store from 1760 to 1770. Later occupants were a milliner, Mary Dickinson, and another merchant, John Lewis. Reconstructed; privately occupied.

Mary Stith Shop—S.

The original of this small reconstructed shop building was owned in the late eighteenth century by Mary Stith, daughter of the Virginia historian, the Reverend William Stith. Now a part of Colonial Williamsburg's exhibition program, it represents the kind of rented quarters in which a music teacher, such as Peter Pelham, might have given lessons. Pelham was among the several musicians who offered instruction in Williamsburg in the art of playing on the harpsichord, violin, flute, French horn, "guittar," and similar instruments.

Hunter's Store—N.

Although this shop appears on the "Frenchman's Map," little is actually

known about it. Historical evidence indicates that it was built sometime after 1772. Operated as a modern shop; reconstructed.

The Printing Office—N.

Here stood the eighteenth-century printing establishment of William Parks, founder of the earliest newspaper in Virginia, "public printer" to the General Assembly, and the colony's first postmaster. Parks also established a paper mill just outside Williamsburg—"the first Mill of the Kind, that ever was erected in this Colony." In this last venture he had the advice and backing of a fellow printer, Benjamin Franklin, who later purchased paper from the mill.

It was on August 6, 1736, that the first issue of the *Virginia Gazette* came off Parks's press here. The files of this weekly—and of its successors and competitors, all of the same name —offer present-day readers a rich account of the life of colonial America, and they have also supplied much information of use in the restoration of Williamsburg. The typographical craftsmanship of William Parks is evident not only in the newspaper, but also in the collected laws of the colony and other books he published.

After Parks's death his foreman, William Hunter, bought the printing shop and succeeded him as public printer, postmaster, and publisher of the *Virginia Gazette*. In 1753 Hunter and Benjamin Franklin were appointed by the British Postmasters-General to be jointly "Deputy Post-

master and Manager" for the whole of British North America. This assignment brought Franklin to visit Hunter in Williamsburg in 1756—when the College of William and Mary conferred an honorary "Degree of A.M." on the Philadelphian.

After Hunter's death in 1761, his son being then a minor, the paper was carried on by Joseph Royle, who died in 1766, and then by John Dixon and Alexander Purdie. In 1775 Purdie established a separate printing office and his own paper, and Dixon was joined by young William Hunter, Jr., a Loyalist, who later supplied the British with military information, fought with Cornwallis at Yorktown, and settled in England after the war.

During excavations at this site several hundred pieces of type, probably of Dutch origin, were unearthed, along with bookbinder's ornaments and crucibles that Parks may have used to melt lead, a lead plate, and lead border ornaments used by Hunter in printing paper money during the French and Indian War. The site is privately owned, and was leased to Colonial Williamsburg to permit

reconstruction of the Printing Office.

Today the building and the one close behind it house a printing shop, branch post office, and bookbindery, all operating as Colonial Williamsburg craft shops.

Orlando Jones House and Office—S.

The T-shaped chimneys and porch chamber to the rear of the house identify this gable-roofed structure with the first quarter of the eighteenth century. Orlando Jones, who owned the original house before his death in 1719, was the son of the Reverend Rowland Jones, first rector of Bruton Parish. Orlando Jones, born in 1681, became a landowner in York and King William counties, and several times represented the latter in the House of Burgesses. His daughter, Frances, and her husband, John Dandridge, were the parents of Martha Washington. The oval garden in the rear, open to the public, is most distinctive. Box hedges, corner seats, and crape myrtle accent the design, and a gnarled paper mulberry tree provides summer shade. The word "office" in

colonial days was applied to any small subsidiary building not otherwise designated as to use. Both buildings are reconstructed and are guesthouses for Williamsburg Inn.

Pitt-Dixon House and The Sign of the Rhinoceros—N.

Like the residence of Orlando Jones across the street, the Pitt-Dixon House is an example of the most common colonial house form in Williamsburg. A shed roof at the rear covers additional first floor space. Wooden grilles at the basement openings are characteristic, although the location of the kitchen in the basement is uncommon. Built about 1717-1719, the original house had as an early owner Christopher de Graffenried, son of the celebrated Swiss baron who deserted the courts of Charles II and Louis XIV to found New Bern, North Carolina. Later a young widow, Sarah Packe, kept a millinery shop here and took lodgers. Still later Dr. George Pitt purchased the property and opened an apothecary shop, The Sign of the Rhinoceros. Visitors who walk

a few steps under the arching live oaks of Colonial Street will see the curved shop window of a small building, the handsome cornice of which echoes that of the main house. Pitt sold the property to the printer John Dixon in 1774. Both buildings are reconstructed and are privately occupied.

INTERSECTION
OF COLONIAL STREET

Prentis Store—N.

This building, a filling station and garage some thirty years ago, is one of Williamsburg's best examples of shop architecture. It was erected in 1740. The original brickwork was revealed after the painstaking removal of numerous coats of paint. For many years the firm of Prentis & Company occupied both this building and an earlier frame store building adjoining it to the east. The shipment of tea that Yorktown patriots dumped into the York River in their own "tea-party" of 1774 was consigned to Prentis & Co. The building houses a retail operation offering craft shop products.

George Reid House—S.

Built between 1789 and 1792 by George Reid, a merchant in Williamsburg, this simple dwelling (formerly known as Captain Orr's) has some unusual architectural design features. The rear cornice has a two-foot overhang that makes a wider roof and thus adds needed space to the second floor. Another pleasing irregularity is the placement of one of the end chimneys inside the house, while the other is outside. A most unusual feature of the interior is an overmantel painting in the parlor depicting an unidentified ruined castle.

Despite the fact that George Reid was obviously a man of influence and a successful merchant in Williamsburg, little is known about him. He was living in the city in 1775 when he was elected an ensign in the Williamsburg militia and secretary of the Williamsburg Society of Freemasons.

An earlier house on this site was occupied in the mid-eighteenth century by Hugh Orr, a blacksmith. In those days a craftsman in Williamsburg had excellent opportunities for marketing his wares to the visiting gentry as well as to the townpeople. Although Orr encountered financial difficulties early in his career, his skill and hard work had enabled him, by the time of his death in 1764, to amass a comfortable estate. In addition to six "Views with gilt frames," a silver teapot, and thirteen tablecloths, his inventory included a library of about forty books. Orr bore the title of captain in the Williamsburg militia, but his tombstone in Bruton churchyard bears only the modest designation "Hammer Man," proclaiming his pride of craft. The restored house is privately occupied.

Ludwell-Paradise House—N.

Built early in the eighteenth century as a town residence of the Ludwell family of Green Spring, this handsome brick mansion was architecturally sophisticated for its day.

Occupancy of the house ultimately devolved to Lucy, second daughter of Philip Ludwell III, although she never owned it. This eccentric lady

lived most of her life in London. Her husband, John Paradise, a scholar and linguist, was a member of Dr. Samuel Johnson's charmed circle of literati.

Lucy Paradise startled London society by such exploits as dashing boiling water from her tea urn on a too garrulous gentleman who annoyed her. Because of her husband's political sympathies, property she owned in Virginia was confiscated by the commonwealth during the Revolution, prompting Dr. Johnson to refer to it as "Paradise's Loss."

In 1805, ten years after her husband's death, Mrs. Paradise returned to take up residence in the house built by her grandfather. Her peculiarities eventually became so marked that she was committed to the state asylum. One of her capricious customs was to entertain callers in a coach, which had been reassembled on a large back porch and was rolled to and fro by a servant during these visits.

Apparently the house was originally intended, like the George Wythe and Lightfoot houses, to have a second floor as deep as the first, with four full rooms; the builders, however, changed their plans and reduced this depth by one-half, covering the rear portion of the first floor by a shed roof. Little repair work was needed to restore the building to its early appearance. The brickwork, a fine example of Flemish bond with headers laid in a pattern, was found to be in excellent condi-

tion. The original framing of massive pieces of hand-hewn timber is exposed in the basement. This was the first property acquired by Mr. Rockefeller and Dr. Goodwin for restoration.

A garden, prized for its dwarf box collection, links the house to the stable and paddock on Nicholson Street. The planting stresses holly, spring bulbs, and summer flowering shrubs. It is open to the public, as is the stable. Other outbuildings include a well, smokehouse, necessary house, and a woodhouse handy to the kitchen. Privately occupied.

William Lightfoot House and Kitchen—S.

The house, to the west, is original and contains a beautifully executed stairway. The building with the clipped gambrel roof was a kitchen, used also as an office; it is reconstructed. In an Act of Assembly of 1769, the boundary between James City and York counties ran "down the middle of the main street to the eastern end of the Market place,

thence into the lane which divides the storehouse of James Anderson merchant, from the lots of the orphan of William Lightfoot, esq. deceased." The orphan was William Lightfoot of Tedington. He was a member of the Virginia House of Delegates from James City County in 1799–1800 and 1805–1806. The property remained in the Lightfoot family until 1839. Both buildings are privately occupied.

The Red Lion—N.

Already known as the Red Lion in 1737, when John Parker obtained a license to operate an ordinary at this location, it still bore the name in 1768. Meanwhile a series of tavernkeepers had found it an ideal situa-

tion near Market Square at which to provide "very good Accommodations for Man and Horse." Along with the Ludwell-Paradise House to the east, this "tenement called the red Lyon where Walter Lenox now lives" was part of the estate of Philip Ludwell III of Green Spring. He died in London in 1767, and this house passed to his daughter Lucy, the eccentric Mrs. Paradise.

The clipped gables of the reconstructed house, often seen in tidewater Virginia, accentuate the robust outside chimneys and add greatly to the beauty of the roof lines. The checkerboard pattern in glazed brick is associated with the early 1700s; the use of rubbed brick to emphasize the structural elements of the walls is here fully exemplified. A basement kitchen, established by archaeological evidence, is an uncommon feature of the house.

The garden, open to the public, has a sunken turf panel with corner seats, a pleached alley, and an aerial hedge of clipped live oaks; it is shaded by tall locusts. Privately occupied.

Peter Hay's Shop—S.

In 1746 Dr. Peter Hay advertised his apothecary shop "adjoining the Market-Place." Ten years later a notice in the *Maryland Gazette* reported that in Williamsburg "On Sunday last betwixt one and two o'Clock in the Day, a Fire broke out in the Shop of Dr. Peter Hay . . . and in less than Half an Hour entirely consumed the same, together with all Medicines,

Utensils, etc. . . . and by the Assistance of a Fire Engine, it was happily prevented from doing any further Damage." Excavations on the site revealed a large chimney foundation and some fragments thought to be the "Utensils" mentioned above.

Over the entrance to attract public notice hangs another of Williamsburg's distinctive signs, in this case a haystack placed between Peter Hay's initials. In an age when many could not read, the astute shopkeeper or tavern proprietor made certain that his premises were clearly marked by a sign for the wayfarer. Reconstructed; privately occupied.

Intersection of Queen Street

Market Square Tavern—S.

In intermittent use as a hostelry during three centuries, the restored Market Square Tavern is today operated in the same capacity by Williamsburg Inn.

The most celebrated colonial lodger was Thomas Jefferson, who rented rooms here from Thomas Craig, tailor, while studying law under the guidance of George Wythe. Gabriel Maupin later purchased the property "for the Purpose of Keeping Tavern," and moved his saddlery and harness-making business here. Patrick Henry was one of his customers for saddles. From about 1775 to about 1791 Maupin also served as keeper of the Magazine—conveniently located next door. Maupin christened his son George Washington, a custom soon to be followed by thousands of his countrymen.

The building offers a good example of the way in which many colonial structures grew gracefully over the years by means of frequent additions. The eastern portion of Market Square Tavern is the earliest and contains a handsome "Great Room" which is completely sheathed and paneled with the original pine in natural finish.

The kitchen yard played an important part as a work area, and the garden provided a pleasant place for games and sociability. The coach house and paddock in the rear no longer provide quarters for blooded coach horses, but the tavern's garden,

with its fruit trees, flowers, and herbs, is still favored by Williamsburg visitors as a place for strolling and relaxation. Sometime after the old Raleigh Tavern burned to the ground in 1859, this hostelry on Market Square became known as the Raleigh Hotel, a name it proudly bore until well into the present century.

Chowning's Tavern—N.

In function as in appearance Chowning's Tavern again takes its place in Williamsburg. Not only has it been rebuilt to resemble an eighteenth-century ordinary, but it is today operated by the Colonial Williamsburg Foundation as an alehouse serving luncheons, garden refreshments, and dinners. Its specialties include Brunswick stew, Welsh rabbit, oysters, clams, hearty sandwiches, and "Chowning's good Bread." Draft ale and beer, a selection of fine wines, and mixed drinks are also served.

In 1766 Josiah Chowning advertised the opening of his tavern "where all who please to favour me with their custom may depend upon the best of entertainment for themselves, servants, and horses, and good pasturage." The rates that could be charged for food and drink were duly fixed each year by the justices of the county, and were ordered to be "openly set up in the public entertaining room of every ordinary." Chowning's Tavern served a less august clientele than the Raleigh or the King's Arms, and good, sturdy, country-made tables and chairs have been selected for today's furnishings.

When weather permits, guests are served in the garden behind the tavern, which is shaded by an arbor of scuppernong grapes. Colonial statutes were explicit in stating that all licensing laws were equally binding out of doors in "booths, arbours and stalls." The kitchen, dairy, and smokehouse have been reconstructed on their original sites in the yard.

THE MAGAZINE AND GUARDHOUSE

A STURDY octagonal building, standing apart in the green expanse of Market Square, the Magazine was the forerunner of today's labyrinthine arsenals. It was erected in 1715 on the urgent request of Governor Alexander Spotswood for a "good substantial house of brick" to house the arms and ammunition dispatched from London by order of Queen Anne for the defense of the royal colony. The governor himself is credited with the design. Sir William Keith, governor of Pennsylvania, who visited Williamsburg, wrote in 1738 that Spotswood "was well acquainted with Figures, and so good a Mathematician, that his Skill in Architecture . . . is yet to be seen in *Virginia,* by the Building of an elegant safe Magazine." The structure has survived to the present day and is now an exhibition building of Colonial Williamsburg.

In colonial times, the Magazine provided an adequate storehouse for the military needs of Virginia. The first line of defense of the colony was the Royal Navy, which convoyed the annual tobacco fleet and maintained one or more men-of-war on the "Virginia Station" in time of stress. But against Indian attacks, local riots, slave insurrections, or even raids by pirates or enemy privateers, the colony depended for its defense upon the relatively untrained and undisciplined militia. Then as now, the protection of hearth and home was recognized as the duty of every freeman. With the exception of certain groups including clergymen, schoolmasters, overseers, and government officials, every able-bodied freeman from twenty-one to sixty was obliged by law to serve in the local militia.

The Magazine assumed added importance during the French and Indian War (1754-1763) when the colony for the first time conducted large-scale military operations on its own soil—the Ohio Valley. At that time, the amount of gunpowder in storage exceeding 60,000 pounds, the people of Williamsburg felt that the Magazine needed further protection. A high wall was accordingly built around it, and provision was made for a guard. A Guardhouse was built close by. Pulled down in the nineteenth century, the wall and the Guardhouse were reconstructed with the aid of archaeological findings, surviving watercolor sketches, and a wood engraving by Benson J. Lossing.

During the night of April 20-21, 1775, the Magazine played its most dramatic role in an incident that did much to precipitate the Revolution in Virginia. In the preceding month the Second Virginia Convention had met in Richmond and had introduced a bill for assembling and training the militia. There Patrick Henry had made the famous declaration: "Is life so dear, or peace so sweet, as to be purchased at the price of chains and slavery? Forbid it, Almighty God! I know not what course others may take, but as for me, give me liberty or give me death."

In Williamsburg Lord Dunmore deemed it wise to have a supply of powder removed from the Magazine, explaining in a letter to London that the action was taken in response to "The series of dangerous measures pursued by the people of this Colony against Government." His orders were carried out by British marines under cover of darkness, but as the governor reported, "tho' it was intended to have been done privately, *Mr. Collins* and his party were ob-

served, and Notice was given immediately to the Inhabitants of this Place; Drums were then sent thro' the City."

Public indignation rose to fever pitch and troops were mustered in various places. Patrick Henry led a party of armed volunteers toward the capital from Hanover County, demanding the return of the powder or payment for it. To this demand the receiver-general of Virginia was constrained to yield; payment was duly made, and the "rebels" dispersed. In somewhat injured tones, Governor Dunmore explained that his only intention had been to forestall the capture of the powder in "an intended insurrection of the slaves"; for this he "certainly rather deserved the thanks of the country than their reproaches." His proclamation, however, did little to calm public sentiment, and an uneasy quiet prevailed. Meanwhile, less than forty-eight hours before the removal of the powder, British troops had fired on Massa-

chusetts irregulars at Lexington. When this news reached Williamsburg ten days later, the *Virginia Gazette* proclaimed in a broadside "the *Sword is now drawn,* and *God* knows when it will be sheathed."

After the Revolution there was no

longer any need for an arsenal at Williamsburg, although the Magazine was pressed into service for powder storage once more by Confederate forces during the Civil War. In other years it was used variously as a market, a Baptist meeting house, a dancing school, and finally as a livery stable.

The Magazine and Guardhouse have been equipped with weapons and furnishings of the period of the French and Indian War.

Within the Magazine military equipment of the eighteenth century is exhibited, including a collection of flintlock muskets—the standard arm of all British and colonial troops. On the bench in the armorer's workshop parts of a typical musket of the 1750s are shown disassembled, together with the armorer's tools. The reconstructed Guardhouse is a typical story-and-a-half brick structure, simply furnished. In the small, brick-paved room on the ground floor a few muskets are racked at one end and soldiers' accouterments are hung.

The Association for the Preservation of Virginia Antiquities, chartered in 1889, made the safeguarding of the Magazine its first project. The Association acquired the Magazine in 1890 and exhibited it for a number of years. In 1946 the A.P.V.A. leased the Magazine to Colonial Williamsburg, which had previously restored it, for exhibition.

COURTHOUSE OF 1770

At THE center of the busy life of Market Square, a courthouse was erected in 1770 to replace an earlier courthouse at the corner of Francis and England streets. This building has stood as a symbol of law and order for nearly two centuries, and served Williamsburg and James City County until 1932. When present plans are carried out, the building will be restored, refurnished, and reopened as a colonial county courthouse, focus of local government in the eighteenth century.

Like many other Virginia courthouses, it is T-shaped. Arched windows and an octagonal cupola add to the official appearance of the building. The design of the overhanging pediment would seem to call for columns, but there is no documentary evidence of their having been ordered. The building is known to have stood without columns until they were added when renovations were undertaken in 1911. In the 1932 restoration, it was therefore decided to return this pediment to its eighteenth-century appearance, and the columns added in 1911 were removed.

Two courts regularly met here—the James City County Court and the municipal court (known as the hustings court). The county court was the principal agent of local government in colonial Virginia, possessed of wide powers, both judicial and executive. Its criminal jurisdiction was restricted to cases not involving "life or member," although an exception was made to allow it to prescribe earcropping for a culprit caught stealing a hog. The hustings court possessed the criminal and civil jurisdiction within the city which the county court exercised elsewhere.

Both the inside and outside of the building have a place in history. Legal notices were posted in front of the Courthouse, and citizens gathered in excitement at its steps to hear announcements of importance. The Declaration of Independence was proclaimed here, with illuminations and the firing of cannon and muskets.

Market Square, the broad green on which the Courthouse is set, was an important center in community life, just as those who planned the city intended. Militiamen were mustered here. Farmers from the countryside used it as a marketplace each Wednesday and Saturday. Twice during the year, on St. George's Day (April 23) and on December 12, a great official town fair was held at the square. Livestock was sold, as well as a bewildering array of other merchandise; there were games, puppet shows, cudgeling matches, beauty contests, cockfights, dancing and fiddling for prizes, and the familiar chase for "A Pig, with the Tail soap'd."

Norton-Cole House—N.

The frame wing of this house is a reconstruction. The brick portion, fronting on Market Square, is original and was completed between 1809 and 1812. It is one of the few nineteenth-century structures preserved by Colonial Williamsburg and is an excellent example of the transitional architecture of the early 1800s. Its masonry work is notably simpler than that of the Ludwell-Paradise House and other neighboring colonial buildings. The *Virginia Gazette* records that fires and robberies beset early tenants, who included a tailor, wigmaker, carpenter, and French baker. Among the owners was John Baker, a noted "surgeon dentist" of colonial America. George Washington, whose teeth—and false teeth—plagued him through life, was a frequent patient of Baker's. The house is named for two other owners: John Hatley Norton of the noted colonial merchant firm of John Norton and Sons of London and Virginia, and Roscow Cole, a nineteenth-century resident who was a merchant in Williamsburg. Privately occupied.

Greenhow-Repiton House and Brick Office—S.

Both the frame house (reconstructed) and the adjacent brick office (restored) were once the property of John Greenhow, whose dwelling and store stood to the west.

A somewhat unconventional appearance is given to this otherwise typical colonial dwelling by the shed-roof additions at the rear and to the east of the building. Reconstruction of the house—destroyed early in the present century—was aided by a watercolor and photographs. The brick

office behind the house was known by local tradition as the Debtors' Prison, but there is no actual evidence of such use. The design and construction make it seem probable that it was used as a shop or residence in colonial days. In 1810 Joseph Repiton, a printer and newspaper publisher, purchased all this property from Greenhow's son. Privately occupied.

Boot and Shoemaker's Shop—S.

This reconstructed building, housing another of Colonial Williamsburg's operating craft shops, occupies the site of the shoemaking establishment of George Wilson & Co. In 1773 Wilson advertised "a choice Cargo of the best Sorts of English Leather for all Manner of Mens Shoes and Pumps, and excellent London Drawlegs for Boots." Today a craftsman again makes shoes with the tools and techniques of the eighteenth century, hand sewing the soles and uppers with "good thread well twisted" and the stitches "hard

"large and commodious Dwelling House" with adjoining store. Greenhow sold china to Patrick Henry for the Palace during Henry's residence there as first governor of the new-born commonwealth. Townspeople are reported to have complained of his high prices. An insurance policy taken out in 1801 indicates that the house followed the contours of the sloping ground and gives its dimensions—large enough to accommodate, a few years later, "a tearing Ball at *Mr.* Greenhow's . . . a six hundred squeeze." This policy, and a description of the house before its destruction in the Civil War, provided by a Williamsburg resident of

drawn with handleathers," as one colonial Virginia statute prescribed. In a twelve-hour working day a good shoemaker could average two pairs of shoes—welted, turned, or stitched. He made them with round, square, or pointed toes, as fashion might decree, but on a straight last—that is, without distinction between right and left—for gentlemen felt that straight shoes presented a more pleasing appearance.

Hanging on the wall of the shop are a number of wooden lasts on which such shoes were formed. Also on display, various kinds of leather and items made of leather—military equipment, fire buckets, and wood carriers, for instance—show the importance of leather to people of an earlier day.

long memory, made possible the reconstruction. Privately occupied.

Greenhow House and Store—S.

John Greenhow, a merchant in Williamsburg from about 1755 until his death in 1787, lived here in a

Greenhow Lumber House—S.

This building, known also as the Spinning and Weaving House, is a part of Colonial Williamsburg's operating craft shop program. It houses a working exhibition of spinning wheels and looms, demonstrated by skilled craftsmen and women. The reconstructed building is of a type used for storing bulky goods, called "lumber" in the eighteenth century.

Flax breaking, spinning flax and wool, and weaving spun threads into plain and patterned textiles are done here as they were carried on in colonial households and later, just before the Revolution, in a commercial workshop. Silks and satins and fine laces were imported, but everyday needs—linens, blankets, and cotton and woolen homespun to clothe the family and servants—were met at home. Industry in these crafts was thought to become a lady, and the mistress of a plantation would spin and weave with the best, teaching the young girls of the family and the slaves. A few itinerant weavers assisted in setting up the looms, but commercial workshops developed only with the exclusion of British goods preceding the Revolution. The Williamsburg Manufactory, the first commercial factory to succeed in eighteenth-century Williamsburg, was established on Capitol Landing Road in 1777.

JAMES GEDDY HOUSE AND SILVERSMITH SHOP

THROUGH some forty mid-eighteenth-century years this property may well have been put to more intensive use in a greater variety of trades and crafts than any other site in the town of Williamsburg. The occupations of gunsmith, founder, cutler, blacksmith, silversmith, jeweler, engraver, watch finisher, milliner, and import merchant were all practiced here at some time during that period—and some of them at the same time.

The principal crafts among them are illustrated here today as part of Colonial Williamsburg's exhibition program. Foundry work, watchmaking, and silversmithing are operating

crafts. In an adjoining shop silver articles may be purchased.

An unusual example of eighteenth-century architecture in Williamsburg, the two-story, L-shaped Geddy House dates from about 1750 and is the only original structure on the site. Its low-pitched roof without dormers and the front porch with balcony and doorway above are also unusual features. The attached shops and separate outbuildings are reconstructed on original foundations.

James Geddy, a gunsmith, was probably located on this corner in an earlier house when he made his initial appearance in the documentary record. The *Virginia Gazette* of July

8, 1737, carried the gunsmith's notice that he would give a reward for the return of a steel crossbow with a broken spring, lost out of his shop in Williamsburg, and that he had on hand "a great Choice of Guns and Fowling-Pieces, of several Sorts and Sizes, true bored, which he will warrant to be good; and will sell them as cheap as they are usually sold in *England*." To another advertisement for his guns he added that he "also makes several Sorts of wrought Brasswork, and casts small Bells."

Seven years later the gunsmith died, leaving his widow with eight children and a claim of £21 8s. 4d. on the colony's government for the cleaning of "Seven Hundred Arms in the Magazine." The oldest boy, David, who had almost certainly been his father's apprentice, succeeded to the business and seems to have taken the third son, William, as his own assistant. A 1751 advertisement declared that these two "Smiths in *Williamsburg*, near the Church, having all manner of Utensils requisite, carry on the Gun-smith's, Cutler's, and Founder's Trade." Not only did they do all kinds of work in these crafts, but they also purveyed "Rupture Bands of different Sorts," a "Vermifuge . . . which safely and effectually destroys all Kinds of Worms in Horses," and cures for "all Diseases incident to Horses."

When his father died, the thirteen-year-old second son, also named James, seems to have already been apprenticed to a silversmith in Williamsburg, perhaps Samuel Galt. At any rate the younger James was well enough established by 1760—being then twenty-nine years old—to purchase this house and lot from his mother. He lived and worked here until 1777, becoming the town's best-known silversmith and often advertising his wares and services in the columns of the *Virginia Gazette*. One notice revealed a concern on Geddy's part that his shop was located so far from the Capitol; the reasonableness of his prices would, he hoped, "remove that Objection of his Shop's being too high up Town . . . and the Walk may be thought rather an Amusement than a Fatigue."

Like others of his calling, Geddy frequently mentioned his readiness to buy old gold and silver, and during the periods of the nonimportation associations before the Revolution, he was careful to say that his goods were country made or had been ordered from England before the association took effect. Among his customers were George Washington, for whom he mended two fans, and Colonel William Preston, for whom he made or mended many silver articles, including a pair of earrings, "the bobbs to be taken back and the money returned if the Lady dont like," and perhaps the brandy warmer now displayed in the shop.

The younger James Geddy also imported and sold jewelry and did watch repairing, advertising that he would fix work of his own that failed within a reasonable time at no expense to the purchaser. He later procured from London a "WATCH FINISHER, who will repair and clean

REPEATING, HORIZONTAL, and PLAIN WATCHES, on reasonable terms." His brother-in-law, William Waddill, also worked in Geddy's shop as a silversmith and engraver. Waddill was commissioned to alter and engrave "Sundry Copper plates for the New Money," and made eight silver handles, sixteen escutcheons, and a large engraved nameplate for the coffin of Governor Botetourt.

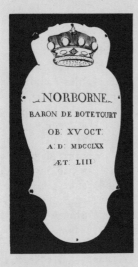

NORBORNE
BARON DE BOTETOURT
OB· XV·OCT·
A·D· MDCCLXX
ÆT· LIII·

The coffin plate is now on display in the Geddy Shop, along with several spoons bearing the touch mark "I·G" of James Geddy. One, with the engraved initials C A A on the handle, presumably those of Christopher and Anne Ayscough, gardener and cook for Governor Fauquier, was found at the site of the Palace kitchen. Others turned up in the course of the archaeological excavation of Geddy's own back yard.

In addition to evidence of several forges, thousands of artifacts were dug up at the Geddy site, among them assorted gun parts, iron-working waste, and slag; unfinished brass castings of shoe buckles and harness buckles, several lead patterns for casting in sand, and much waste brass; many watch glass fragments, some watch keys, and clock parts, including a very fine spandrel for a clock dial; sword parts, and other possible remains of cutlery operations; pieces of marble and tile, iron hinges, brass latches (two stamped with David Geddy's initials), locks and keys, and the like; and great quantities of glass and ceramic fragments, some of very high quality, suggestive of the touches of luxury that a successful craftsman like James Geddy, Jr., could enjoy in his own home.

For Geddy was not just a tradesman, but also a leader of his community. Like his fellow artisans, he belonged to the "middling" class, which owned property, enjoyed the rights of all Englishmen, and could vote for the city's representatives in the House of Burgesses. Indeed, Geddy himself was one of three artisans named to the Williamsburg common council. In 1775, along with some of Williamsburg's most substantial citizens, he was appointed to a "Committee to represent the City" in furthering the patriot cause.

The furnishings presently placed in Mr. Geddy's house are largely of American colonial rather than of English origin, and are of a quality to

reflect his economic and social standing. One item, the spinet, recalls his
daughter Anne's accomplishments at
the keyboard. A poem that appeared
anonymously in the *Virginia Gazette*
of December 20, 1768, discloses the
effect she had on one admirer. The
first stanza of his effort, entitled "On
Miss Anne Geddy singing, and playing on the Spinet," will suffice here:

When Nancy on the spinet plays
  I fondly on the virgin gaze,
And wish that she was mine;
Her air, her voice, her lovely face,
Unite with such excessive grace,
  That nymph appears divine!

Visitors to the Geddy Shop will be
interested in the unusual collection of
watches and watchmaker's tools presented by Edward P. Hamilton of Mil-
ton, Massachusetts.

INTERSECTION OF PALACE GREEN

Custis-Maupin House—S.

John Custis owned the original of
this house, or tenement, as a house
to rent was called in the eighteenth
century. Various stages of growth are
discernible: it was first enlarged by a
one-and-one-half story wing to the
west, then by another addition behind that. This earlier house was
replaced when, about 1840, John M.
Maupin built a "handsome house on
the site of an old ruinous building
opposite the lower corner of the
churchyard." Reconstructed; privately
occupied. The garden is open to the
public.

BRUTON PARISH CHURCH

At the corner of Duke of Gloucester Street and Place Green, Bruton Parish Church stands as a strong link between the past and the present. From 1715 to the present time this building has been in continuous use, a fine architectural example of the colonial church in America, and a reminder in bricks and mortar of the part religion played in the daily life of eigh-teenth-century Virginia. It was a rector of this parish, the late Reverend W. A. R. Goodwin, who first conceived the restoration of Williamsburg and interested Mr. John D. Rockefeller, Jr., in the project. Together they shared the leadership and development of the work.

Bruton Parish was formed in 1674 by merging two earlier parishes (one of them founded in 1633), and it was named for an English parish in Somerset from which several leading parishioners came, among them Thomas Ludwell, secretary of Virginia. A new church was ordered built at Middle Plantation in 1677 on land given by Colonel John Page. Completed in 1683, the small, buttressed brick church in Jacobean style was big enough for a rural parish; with the establishment of the College and the removal of the capital from Jamestown to Williamsburg, however, it soon became inadequate, the parishioners "often outed of their places." Accordingly, Governor Spotswood in 1711 presented the vestry with a "draught" for a new church and the Assembly appropriated £200 to help defray the cost.

The present church was begun that year, close by the old, and was completed in 1715. The vestry set aside a large square pew for the use of the governor and the Council. The governor was also provided with a canopied chair. During sessions of the Assembly the transept pews were reserved for burgesses.

Church and state were united in colonial Virginia, and officeholders under the crown were obliged to conform to the established church. All classes of colonists, from great planters to the humblest artisan and slave, participated in the sacraments of the Anglican church. The stone font, according to tradition brought from the church at Jamestown, probably witnessed the baptism of fourteen slaves listed in the name of George Washington. Since the Virginia aristocracy was politically minded, most of the leading planters became members of the Assembly and, as such, worshipped in Bruton Parish

Church. During times of political crisis, the aid of God was humbly sought: in 1774, when word reached Williamsburg that Parliament had closed the port of Boston, the burgesses set aside a day for fasting, humiliation, and prayer, and went to Bruton in a body "to implore the divine interposition, for averting the heavy Calamity which threatens destruction to our Civil Rights, and the Evils of civil War."

The chancel of the church was extended twenty-five feet to the east in 1752; three years later an organ from England was installed in a loft probably at the western end. The first organist, who served for forty-three years, was Peter Pelham, stepbrother of the Boston artist, John Singleton Copley. Since Pelham was also keeper of the Gaol, he habitually and conveniently brought a prisoner to pump the organ.

The walls and windows of the church are original, but much of the interior woodwork was torn out during the nineteenth century; the old high pews were cut down, the colonial pulpit was discarded, and the west end was partitioned off as a Sunday school room. The Victorian taste of the 1800s was even responsible for the introduction of plush-bottomed, spurious Gothic chairs. The interior, partially restored in 1905

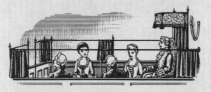

and more completely in 1938, once again resembles its eighteenth-century appearance.

The west gallery is original. It was originally set aside for the use of students at the College, whose initials are still discernible carved in the handrail. The north transept gallery was used by slaves, and was at one time entered by an outside stairway. The south gallery was built in 1720 by the then speaker of the House of Burgesses at his own expense.

It was considered an honor in colonial times to be buried within the confines of the church. Among the gravestones which can be seen there is that of the royal governor, Francis Fauquier, to whom Jefferson paid tribute as "the ablest man" who ever filled the office.

The main portion of the church is symmetrical; chancel and nave are equal. The use of arched doors and both round and arched windows is typical of colonial churches in Vir-

ginia. The brick is a light salmon color, laid in Flemish bond, with glazed headers set in a checkerboard pattern. In 1769 a new tower was built of darker brick, with far fewer glazed headers set in no particular pattern. Capped by stout molded brick, the wall that encloses the churchyard dates from 1754. The roof of the church is steep, and the rake boards at the gables taper in width as they ascend, creating the impression of an even steeper pitch. This soaring quality is climaxed in the emphatic vertical of the tower, surmounted by the wooden steeple. In it hangs a bell, presented to the parish by James Tarpley in 1761, which has rung out on many occasions in the last two hundred years. Today, still administered by its vestry, this Episcopal church continues its long tradition of community service.

Hartwell Perry's Ordinary—S.

The appearance of the building where Hartwell Perry once kept an ordinary was recorded in a watercolor, painted in 1834 by Thomas Millington, son of an engineer and science professor at the College. Ar-

chaeological evidence has confirmed his accuracy. Perry was the owner from about 1782 until his death in 1800. An earlier occupant was John Spiers, "joyner and cabinet-maker," who leased the property from Colonel Custis in 1744, promising to keep the premises in good condition and "the Chimneys clean swept at all times to prevent danger of fire." Another cabinetmaker, Peter Scott, rented a shop here from 1755 to 1771 and lived next door to the east.

The sign before the house may at first puzzle the visitor. In fact it is, like Peter Hay's sign, a rebus: Hart is another word for deer, and perry is a drink made from pears. Reconstructed; privately occupied.

Taliaferro-Cole Shop and Pulaski Club—S.

Only the street front of this colonial shop required restoration. The work was simplified by Millington's painting, which showed the shop and the buildings on either side. The distinctive and unusually long shed roof was extended far beyond the outer wall to shelter a nearby well. The shop was built before 1782 probably by Charles Taliaferro (pronounced Tolliver). In 1804 it was purchased by Jesse Cole along with the house next door. He used the smaller building as a post office and general store. A plaque set in the ground in front of the shop commemorates the Pulaski Club, an informal discussion group of long standing that still meets here. It was named for the Polish count who fought and died for American independence.

The Taliaferro-Cole shop currently houses one of Colonial Williamsburg's craft operations, the vital art of coopering. Barrels and kegs of various shapes and sizes were the common containers for storing and shipping all kinds of goods—from boots to brandy —in the eighteenth century. The tobacco hogshead, 48 inches high and 30 inches in diameter, was perhaps the commonest in colonial Virginia. Tubs, buckets, and other open containers made of staves likewise came from the cooper's skilled hand. The trade was so necessary that most large plantations included a cooper among the work force. Here again the visitor can watch as a skilled craftsman makes, wholly by hand and eye, casks of many sorts.

Taliaferro-Cole House—S.

Charles Taliaferro, well-known coachmaker-merchant, is believed to have occupied this house soon after 1760. He also owned fourteen lots in Williamsburg, a large tract of land in the country, and a "brewhouse" and warehouse on Archer's Hope Creek at College Landing, one of the two shallow-water "ports" of the city. Among other activities, Taliaferro controlled several small, flatbottomed river boats, manned by Negro crews, which were employed in coastal trade on the bay and river. In 1779 he offered for sale at the warehouse salt, tar, barreled pork, hog's lard, bacon, shad and herring, coal, pine plank, and cypress boards. A census of 1783 noted that Taliaferro had eleven slaves, five horses, and four cattle.

In 1804 the property was purchased by Jesse Cole, whose descendants occupied the house until recently. The house and outbuildings, which lie along Nassau Street, form an L, a general plan similar to that of the George Wythe property. Except for the unusual front porch, which was reconstructed according to marks revealed by antique weatherboards, the house is restored. It is privately occupied; the garden is open to the public.

INTERSECTION OF NASSAU STREET

Bryan House—S.

The A-roof house built on this site about the middle of the 1700s survived until early in the present century, being used in the intervening years as a grocery store, residence, and school. It was owned at the end of the eighteenth century by a family named Bryan. The architects were guided in the work of reconstruction by a few photographs that were found, and by residents who recalled the appearance of the house. The garden has a formal arrangement of clipped box hedges and topiary work. It includes the customary fruit trees as well as a handsome arbor and a sheltered bench. The garden is open to the public; the house is privately occupied.

Blaikley-Durfey House and Durfey Shop—S.

Catherine Blaikley, described in the *Virginia Gazette* as "an eminent Midwife . . . who, in the course of her Practice, brought upwards of three thousand Children into the World," died in 1771 at the age of "73 Years and Upwards," after long residence in Williamsburg. William Blaikley owned this site as early as 1734 and would seem to have been living here when he died in 1736, leaving his "lands, houses, negroes, goods and chattels" to his "loving wife, Catherine." The inventory of his estate listed the items in each of the rooms in such a way as to suggest the interior plan of the house. Slaves belonging to Mrs. Blaikley were baptized in Bruton Parish Church in 1748.

In 1773 Severinus Durfey, a tailor, announced his removal to the house lately occupied by Mrs. Blaikley, and at the same time took occasion to plead with all who were "indebted to him for more than twelve Months . . . to pay off their Balances." The building thought to have been Durfey's shop appeared in the Millington

sketch that showed Hartwell Perry's Ordinary. The golden fleece signboard was an emblem often used by tailors.

Both buildings are reconstructed and both are privately occupied. The garden in the rear is typical of the small house gardens of the city and is open to the public.

John Blair House—N.

Here lived John Blair, Jr., scion of a family already distinguished for two generations. The first member to come to the colony was the Reverend James Blair, commissary in Virginia for the bishop of London and later founder and first president of the College of William and Mary. His brother, Dr. Archibald Blair, followed from Scotland in 1690. A physician and merchant, Archibald long served as vestryman and burgess. Archibald's son John also served as burgess and was auditor-general of the colony from 1728 to 1771. In 1745 he was appointed a councillor, Governor Gooch explaining to the authorities in London that he had not earlier recommended this step because "during his Uncle's the late Commissary's lifetime, he was in narrow Circumstances." With an inheritance of "near ten Thousand Pound" from his uncle, Blair was felt to be well enough established for the honor. Later, as president of the Council, he twice served as acting governor of Virginia.

John Blair, Sr., may well have lived in this house; certainly his son John did. John Blair, Jr., graduated from

William and Mary, studied at the Middle Temple, London, and himself became a burgess and later clerk of the Council. He was on the committee that drew up Virginia's Declaration of Rights and first state constitution, and he served the new commonwealth as councillor, judge, and chief justice. In 1787 he represented Virginia at the Constitutional Convention, where he firmly advocated federal union. President Wash-

ington appointed him, in 1789, to the United States Supreme Court, where he served until his retirement to Williamsburg in 1796. Blair died in 1800.

The restored house has early type hipped dormers and the original stone steps imported from England. The kitchen, with its huge chimney, is reconstructed. Between the kitchen and the street is a small, formal herb garden, open to the public. Both buildings are privately occupied.

Merchants Square, a business and shopping district, extends from the John Blair House to the intersection of Boundary Street. It is not a part of the Historic Area, but the buildings have been designed in eighteenth- and nineteenth-century styles.

THE COLLEGE OF WILLIAM
AND MARY

A VISITOR who stands at the college gate, at the western end of Duke of Gloucester Street, will see at once that the orderly and almost symmetrical area of the college yard is an architectural unit in itself. The central structure is the Wren Building, with its massive chimneys and lofty cupola. Flanking it at the north and south are the President's House and the Brafferton, buildings apparently identical in dimension and detail, although the Brafferton is actually somewhat smaller. These two buildings have narrow, many-paned windows and steep-pitched roofs, to give a strong balancing vertical accent to the architectural composition.

The College of William and Mary was chartered in 1693 as an Anglican college "to the end that the Church of Virginia may be furnish'd with a Seminary of Ministers of the Gospel, and that the Youth may be piously educated in good Letters and Manners, and that the Christian Faith may be propagated amongst the Western Indians, to the Glory of Almighty God." Throughout the colonial period William and Mary was the center of higher education in Virginia and Maryland; both the tobacco colonies of the Chesapeake were taxed to finance its construction. It is the second oldest college in the United States.

In the eighteenth century, long before Horace Mann and the great public-school movement, education was not easily come by in the colonies. There were a few endowed schools in Virginia, such as the Symmes-Eaton Academy of Elizabeth City

County and "Matty Whaley's School" in Williamsburg; often a clergyman ran a small school to serve his parish and augment his income; and the College itself had a grammar school. Sons of plantation owners, who commonly were entrusted to tutors at home for their schooling, could either attend William and Mary or go overseas to Oxford, Cambridge, or Edinburgh, or to read law at the Inns of Court in London. Higher education conferred considerable prestige on the few who attained it. Girls had little formal education.

Although the average enrollment at William and Mary was less than one hundred during the eighteenth century, the college exerted great influence on the intellectual life of Virginia and produced an extraordinary number of distinguished alumni, including Thomas Jefferson, James Monroe, and John Marshall. Four of the first ten presidents of the United States were associated with the College. George Washington was chancellor for eleven years. Edmund Randolph, Washington's attorney general,

wrote: "Until the revolution, most of our leading [men] were the alumni of William and Mary."

The faculty included such distinguished men as the Reverend Hugh Jones, mathematician and grammarian, Dr. William Small, physicist, and George Wythe, jurist and classics teacher. "I know of no place in the world," wrote Jefferson in 1788, "while the present professors remain, where I would so soon place a son." In 1729 there were six professors in the three schools of Humanity, Philosophy, and Divinity. It was largely through the influence of alumnus Jefferson that the curriculum was broadened in 1779. To the old professorships of moral philosophy, natural philosophy, and mathematics were added new chairs of law and police, chemistry and medicine, ethics and belles lettres, and modern languages. The chair of divinity was discontinued as was the grammar school. William and Mary had been founded as an Anglican college, but, as the Reverend James Madison, president of the College, explained, "it is now thought that Establishments in favor of any particular Sect are incompatible with the Freedom of a Republic."

Wren Building

This is the oldest academic edifice in English-speaking America in continuous use. It became also (1928-1931) the first major Williamsburg structure to be restored by Mr. John D. Rockefeller, Jr., although remaining an integral part of the College. Several of the building's first- and second-floor rooms have been carefully furnished as they might have been in the eighteenth century, and, along with the Chapel, are open to the public the year round. Through the cooperation of the state government and the College authorities, Colonial Williamsburg is pleased to exhibit these facilities. The building also continues in daily use for classes and faculty offices, as well as for ceremonial and other contemporary purposes.

The visitor entering the Wren Building by the main (east) door and passing through the central corridor to the "piazza" will see on the walls a number of plaques commemorating achievements in peace and war of the College's faculty, students, and alumni, as well as its own academic "firsts."

The courtyard was originally intended to be enclosed within a quadrangular building, the two wings being joined across the far ends by a structure similar to the first side. Thomas Jefferson, an accomplished amateur architect, drew plans for an enlarged quadrangle, and foundations had been laid when the outbreak of the Revolution put an end to the project. Some of those foundations are still under the surface of the ground.

Known through most of its life simply as "the College," the Wren Building now bears the name of the distinguished English architect who may have shaped its original design. According to an early account, it was "first modelled by Sir Christopher Wren," but was "adapted to the Nature of the Country by the Gentlemen there." The cornerstone was laid in 1695, and although fires in 1705, 1859, and again in 1862 did serious damage, the massive exterior walls are largely original. They have withstood not only the flames but also the architectural modifications and structural alterations that were part of each rebuilding. The building now has the outward appearance it showed from about 1716 (except for the Chapel wing) until 1859.

Added in 1732, the Chapel is evidence that in colonial Virginia the established Church of England played a central role in education as well as in government. Students in all four branches of the College (grammar school, Indian school, school of philosophy, and school of divinity) began the day at 6 or 7 o'clock with morning prayer service in the Chapel and ended it with evening prayer or evensong. On occasion outstanding students would deliver moral discourses after the evening service to an audience of both town and gown, and the Chapel was the setting for conferring of degrees. (It is used today for some community religious services and is the scene of many weddings.)

In the crypt below the Chapel lie buried Sir John Randolph, his sons Peyton and John "the Tory," Governor Botetourt, Bishop James Madison, and several other distinguished Virginians.

The grammar school of the College of William and Mary admitted boys of about twelve who spent four years in the intensive study of Latin and Greek as well as mathematics, geography, and penmanship. Emphasis was laid on written themes and oral declamations, usually in Latin and based on the classical Greek and Latin authors. After morning prayer in the Chapel and breakfast in the Great Hall, the grammar school sat from 7 to 11 a.m. and again, after midday dinner, from 2 until 5 p.m. when evening prayer was said. A light supper followed, and the day ended when the whole student body gathered before the masters to be counted, blessed, and sent to bed at 9 o'clock. Probably no more than forty boys attended the grammar school at any time before the Revolution.

It was in the school of philosophy that Jefferson enrolled at the age of seventeen and studied for two years, probably in the room that has now been refurnished in the style of English schoolrooms of the time. Up to thirty young men studied logic, rhetoric, and ethics in this lecture room for moral philosophy. Lectures in natural philosophy—mathematics, physics, and metaphysics—were given in another room at the opposite end of the building. A student who successfully completed four years of study, submitted a written thesis, and made an oral defense of it received the Bachelor of Arts degree. He could then proceed to a Master of Arts, enter the divinity school, or begin the study of law with a practicing attorney or at the Inns of Court in London.

The Great Hall was the commons, or dining room, for the entire College. The president, the professors, and the master of the grammar school ate at the head table. At the other tables, in descending order of status, sat the students, lesser faculty, "servitors and college officers," and finally the Indian master and his pupils. From the kitchen, directly below, the housekeeper saw to it that "plenty of Victuals" were "served up in the cleanest and neatest Manner possible" thrice a day. Beer, cider, and "toddy, or spirits with water" were also provided.

The House of Burgesses met in the Great Hall during the years 1700 to 1704 while the Capitol was under construction, and again in 1747-1752 while the burned-out Capitol was being rebuilt. On the first occasion the government of Governor Nicholson crowded all its activities and offices into the building, "to the great disturbance of the College business," President Blair complained. At another time he told a visitor, "Here we sometimes preach and pray, and sometimes fiddle and dance; the one to edify, and the other to divert us." The Great Hall served also a chapel, before the Chapel wing was built, and as a College ballroom.

In addition to the Grammar School Room and the Moral Philosophy Room on the first floor, two rooms on the second have been refurnished and opened to public visit. The Professors' Common Room would today be called the faculty lounge or library. Here the professors and masters, each of whom had his own study and bedroom in the College, could gather for relaxing conversation and refreshments. In it the College's "philosophical apparatus" might be kept safe from pilferage. Here the students assembled each evening for roll call before going to their own quarters on the second and third floors.

The Convocation Room, familiarly known to generations of college students as the Blue Room, was the focal point of the College administration. In the eighteenth century the president and masters met here to conduct College business, the College's charter and seal were kept here, and students were summoned to this awesome sanctum to be commended or censured for their academic (and extracurricular) behavior. The room is still used for meetings of the Board of Visitors and Governors of the College.

An archaeological exhibit that is open to the public is displayed in the basement.

President's House—N.

Built in 1732-1733, this house has been the residence of every president of the College of William and Mary. Its first occupant was the Reverend James Blair, the energetic Anglican clergyman from Scotland who first induced the Virginia Assembly to favor the erection of a college and then, in 1693, persuaded King William and Queen Mary to charter and endow it. He also supervised the construction of all the early buildings and selected the first faculty and curriculum. Blair served as president for half a century. During the last stages of the Revolution, the house was used briefly as headquarters by Cornwallis. French officers serving under Rochambeau occupied it after the siege of Yorktown, causing accidental damage by fire which was repaired at the expense of the French government.

The philosopher and scientist James Madison lived here as president of the College (1777-1812). In 1790 he became the first Episcopal bishop of Virginia.

The Brafferton—S.

When Robert Boyle, the noted British scientist, died in 1691, he left his personal property to charitable and pious uses at the discretion of his executors. They invested some of the funds in the manor of Brafferton in Yorkshire. President James Blair persuaded them to give the profits from Brafferton to the College to be used for the education and conversion of Indian boys—except for £90 a year to be sent to Harvard College for the same purpose. At first the Indians had a classroom in the Wren Building and were quartered elsewhere in the town, but in 1723 this building was completed for their use. Until the Revolution cut off revenue from the Boyle foundation, there were always some—often a dozen or more—Indians at the college, although most of them seem to have forgotten their prayers and catechism when they left Williamsburg. So far as is known, not one of these Indians became a missionary as Boyle's executors had hoped.

The Brafferton today provides offices and guest rooms for College alumni. The building suffered remarkably little damage over the years, although during the Civil War its interior woodwork was ripped from the walls by Federal troops and used for firewood.

Francis and France Streets — East to West

Benjamin Waller House and Office—S.

This L-shaped colonial house with gambrel-roofed wing was built and several times added to over the period 1745 to 1770 by Benjamin Waller, a prominent Williamsburg attorney who was George Wythe's law teacher. In an impressive career, Waller held a variety of offices: he served as burgess, city recorder, judge of the court of admiralty, and vestryman of Bruton Parish. The property, which remained in his family for over a century, was subsequently owned and occupied by his grandson, William Waller, who married Elizabeth Tyler, daughter of President John Tyler. The office, adjacent to the house on Francis Street, was

probably used by the original owner, Benjamin Waller, in his law practice. Behind the house lies a formal garden, open to the public, recreated following a sketch probably drawn in the 1790s. The restored house and reconstructed office are both privately occupied.

Draper House—N.

This long, narrow, house-and-shop combination is admirably located on a corner of the Capitol Square. John Draper, a farrier and smith who owned the property in the late eighteenth century, undoubtedly profited greatly because of his strategic site.

During the Revolution Draper helped to haul guns and general supplies for the "public service." Reconstructed; privately occupied.

Basset Hall—S.

This handsome, two-story building, to be seen from the entrance of the long driveway, is a good example of a small plantation house set off by outbuildings, gardens, and a fine, tree-shaded approach. It was erected sometime before 1766 by Colonel Philip Johnson, a burgess who suffered financial reverses and soon afterward was forced to rent the house as a tavern. About 1800 the property was purchased by Colonel Burwell Bassett, Martha Washington's nephew. Among the galaxy of guests who visited the hospitable Colonel Bassett was the Irish poet Thomas Moore, who is said to have composed "To a Firefly" after watching lightning bugs in the gardens one summer evening. Partially restored; privately occupied.

Carter-Moir House and Moir Shop—N.

In 1745 John Carter "obtain'd a License to retale Liquors," and advertised in the *Gazette* to give "Notice to all Persons who are desirous of cheap Entertainment, that they may be supply'd with good Pasture. . . . Also good Lodging, either private or publick." By 1777 James Moir occupied the buildings on this property. A tailor by trade, he was also willing to accommodate students

from Mr. Maury's grammar school in "Capitol square" nearby, proposing "to lodge, board, wash, and

mend for them, at a very low price." Both reconstructed buildings are privately occupied.

Semple House—S.

This restored house is a harbinger of the Federal style of architecture that followed the Revolution. Although built before 1782, the classical influence—soon to be felt throughout the young republic—is evident in the porch with its carefully molded columns, elaborate cornice, and enriched pediment. The house was owned by James Semple, judge and professor of law at the College. In

1801 Semple insured "four buildings on a Back street South of the old Capitol." A sketch of the house facade and five outbuildings, with dimensions, was attached. Measurements of the house, shown in this sketch almost exactly as it appears today, were given as "24 feet by 22 feet Two Stories high" with two wooden wings, 22 feet by 20, one story high. The dependencies described, all one-story wooden buildings, were a kitchen 16 by 16 feet, a smokehouse 12 by 12 feet, an office (really two separate buildings, one 20 by 16, the other 12 by 12), and a stable and carriage house 20 by 40 feet. In addition, excavations revealed the founda-

tions of a dairy, well, and garden walks. The small building just east of the dwelling house is original. Privately occupied.

Ayscough House—N.

In this craft shop, a reconstructed house, a skilled gunsmith makes and mends flintlock firearms. His muskets, fowling pieces, rifles, and rifled pistols are exact replicas of the same kinds of weapons carried by colonial Vir-

ginians. He uses the same careful hand methods and hand tools as did his predecessors.

Eighteenth-century Williamsburg craftsmen often pieced out the income from their primary specialties by carrying on a second trade or related craft. Silversmiths often did jewelry work, shoemakers engaged in cobbling, and innkeeping supplemented the incomes of all sorts of craftsmen. The colonial gunsmith, however, had to be skilled in several specialties to start with. Forging the barrel of a gun was blacksmith's work; making the lock required the fine techniques of the clockmaker; shaping and finishing the stock called for the skills of the woodcarver; and adding the customary silver or brass ornamentation demanded all the artistry and mastery of silversmith, brazier, and engraver.

The original building here was purchased in 1768 by Christopher Ayscough and his wife, presumably from funds left her by Governor Fauquier in appreciation of her faithful and efficient management of his kitchen. Christopher Ayscough was gardener at the Palace. The Ayscoughs operated the house briefly as a small tavern.

INTERSECTION OF BLAIR STREET

Nelson-Galt House—N.

This house, one of the oldest in Williamsburg, was built before 1718 by William Robertson. By 1749 it was owned by William Nelson, at one time president of the Council, and later by his even more distinguished son Thomas, a signer of the Declaration of Independence.

Thomas Nelson commanded Virginia's forces in the Yorktown campaign and succeeded Jefferson as governor, but illness forced his retirement. He died in 1789, having sacrificed his health and a very large portion of his considerable fortune in the cause of independence. In 1823 the house was sold to the Galt family, notable citizens of Williamsburg since colonial days. Their

descendants have lived here ever since. The small office close to the front of the lot is also original, with some restoration. House and office are both privately occupied.

Chiswell-Bucktrout House—S.

The roof line of this reconstructed dwelling is unusual in Williamsburg although it was common in England at the beginning of the eighteenth century, the period when the house was built. The original form was established by a study of roof timbers and numbered beams in the surviving portions of the building. The owner, Colonel John Chiswell, was in 1766 the center of a controversy that "put the whole country into a ferment." Arrested for killing a Scottish merchant in a fit of rage, he was released on bail, an unusually lenient procedure that the less privileged attributed to his political and family connections. The Colonel died just before his trial—by his own hand, it was rumored. Benjamin Bucktrout, cabinetmaker and merchant, purchased the house in

1774. A guesthouse for Williamsburg Inn with public gardens.

Providence Hall—S.

This eighteenth-century house, standing well back from the street, was moved to Williamsburg from its previous location at Providence Forge, Virginia. Outside of the Historic Area, it is privately occupied.

Ewing House—S.

Peter Moyer, a baker, either built or added to the house on this lot about 1788. Later it belonged to Ebenezer Ewing, a merchant who had emigrated from Scotland and died in 1795. He left the house to Elizabeth Ashton, mother of his son

Thomas, with the proviso that "the moment she marries . . . it becomes the property of my son." Some years later, Thomas was bound out "to learn art of seaman or mariner," and disappeared during his apprenticeship. Restored; the Ewing House and Forge are Williamsburg Inn guesthouses.

Dr. Barraud House—N.

An example of symmetry in colonial architecture, this comfortable dwelling was erected about 1780 and incorporates earlier buildings on the

site. A massive gabled roof surmounts a typical Virginia house plan, with two rooms on either side of a central hall. The light green of the cornice and porch is the original paint color found when the house was studied prior to restoration. The porch railing shows the Chinese influence prevalent in the second half of the eighteenth century.

The early owner of the house was Dr. Philip Barraud, a public-spirited physician, active in the affairs of the college and of Eastern State Hospital. He left Williamsburg in 1799 to become superintendent of the Marine Hospital in Norfolk, and his house was sold in 1801 to Mrs. Anna Byrd, the widow of Otway Byrd. Privately occupied.

Moody House—S.

Josias Moody owned this unpretentious house from the 1790s until his death about 1810. Archaeological evidence indicates that it was built before 1750 and was altered several times, reaching its present size and appearance by 1782. There is a long lean-to roof on the south, usually an indication that additions were made to an earlier structure. Restored; the Moody House and Kitchen are guesthouses for Williamsburg Inn.

Orrell House—S.

In this, an otherwise typical gambrel-roof house, the entrance hall is

not centered; all the living quarters are therefore to one side of the hall. The house, probably built during the third quarter of the eighteenth century and now restored, takes its name from John Orrell or Orrill, who owned it about 1800. Both it and the Orrell Kitchen are guesthouses for Williamsburg Inn.

Lewis House—N.

Reconstructed. Originally part of the Orlando Jones property, which extended from Duke of Gloucester Street to Francis Street, the lot was separated after 1790 and came into the possession of one Charles Lewis, who owned it until 1806 and is believed to have built the original house. It is a guesthouse for Williamsburg Inn. The garden is open to the public.

INTERSECTION OF
COLONIAL STREET

Williamsburg Inn—S.

A modern hotel of over 200 rooms, the Inn is designed after the manner of resort architecture of the early nineteenth century, and contrasts with the colonial architecture of the Historic Area. Many restored and reconstructed colonial houses and kitchens in the Historic Area are operated as guest facilities of the Inn—as are the modern suites and executive meeting rooms of the Providence Hall wings. The sports area to the south of the Inn includes an 18-hole championship golf course, a 9-hole short course, clubhouse, tennis courts, swimming pools, bowling green, and croquet court. The dining room, lounge, and clubhouse grill are open to the public for meals and beverages.

The Quarter—S.

Little is known of this small, quaint, late eighteenth-century cottage, although it is believed to have served for a time as slave quarters to the adjoining property. The front portion of the restored house is typical of the 16-by-24-foot dwelling of the early 1700s. The addition of a shed portion at the rear has created an unusual and attractive roof line. A guesthouse for Williamsburg Inn.

Bracken-Carter House—S.

Reverend John Bracken of Bruton Parish Church owned a good deal of land along Francis Street, including this lot. On maps dating from the early nineteenth century it is marked "Js. Carter," and records show that in 1804 Elizabeth Carter was living here. The architecture of the reconstructed house is characteristic of the mid-1700s. A guesthouse for Williamsburg Inn.

Bracken House—S.

Two large T-shaped chimneys, characteristic of the early eighteenth century, lend weight to the design of this typical Virginia house. The steep gable roof is accented at the eaves by fine modillion cornices.

Reverend John Bracken owned the

house for many years, although there is no evidence that he lived here. Bracken became rector of Bruton Parish in 1773, soon after his arrival from England. He continued in that office for forty-five years, until his death, and in addition was mayor of Williamsburg in 1800. He was elected bishop of Virginia in 1812 but declined consecration, presumably on account of his age and many local commitments, which included holding the presidency of the College from 1812 to 1814. Through his marriage in 1776 to Sally Burwell of Carter's Grove, a great plantation near Williamsburg, he was related to many leading families in Virginia and acquired considerable wealth. For many years he occupied, and ultimately bought, the Lightfoot House. The restored Bracken House and the Bracken Kitchen are guesthouses for Williamsburg Inn.

Masonic Lodge—N.

This modern building is privately owned, and was erected by the Williamsburg Masons on the site of an eighteenth-century meeting place of this same lodge. Among early members were Peyton Randolph, Edmund Randolph, James Monroe, Bishop James Madison, St. George Tucker, and Peter Pelham. The "Masonic Kitchen" is a guesthouse for Williamsburg Inn.

INTERSECTION OF
QUEEN STREET

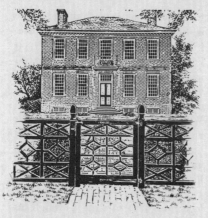

Lightfoot House—S.

Architectural evidence indicates that the house was originally a two and one-half story double tenement built about 1730. The house was brought to its present form during the 1750s. This substantial change suggests that the Lightfoots converted the earlier house from a rental property to a townhouse. It is believed that Colonel Philip Lightfoot, a wealthy Yorktown merchant and planter, owned the property early in the eighteenth century. In 1783 Philip Lightfoot of Caroline County advertised the house for sale. It was described as "a large two-story brick dwelling house with four rooms on a floor . . . lying on the back street near to the market." The Reverend John Bracken, rector of Bruton Parish Church, bought the house and lots in 1786.

This fine residence, with brick walls laid in Flemish bond, is unusual in having a second floor as high as the first. The house is adorned by a ro-bust course in molded brick and by a wrought iron balcony suggestive of the balcony at the Palace. The decorative front fence shows Chinese influence; to the east, separating the orchard from the service area, is a wattled fence made of vines. The outbuildings, some of a distinctive dusky red color, have been reconstructed on colonial foundations. The Lightfoot Kitchen and the Lightfoot Laundry are guesthouses for Williamsburg Inn. The mansion itself has been tastefully furnished with fine antiques and is equipped with modern conveniences in order to serve as an appropriate guesthouse for distinguished visitors to Williamsburg.

Lightfoot Tenement—S.

The term "tenement" in the eighteenth century meant simply a rented house. This was one of the seven adjoining properties that William Lightfoot sold to the Reverend John Bracken in 1786. It has been reconstructed as a shop-type building with clipped gambrel roof and is a guesthouse for Williamsburg Inn. The garden is open to the public.

INTERSECTION OF
SOUTH ENGLAND STREET

Nicholas-Tyler Office—S.

The original of this small, reconstructed building was probably erected by Robert Carter Nicholas after he

acquired the property in 1770. The site is part of the property on which the James City County Courthouse was built in 1715. Roscow Cole owned it from 1819 to 1835, and used a small building which stood here as an office. Privately occupied.

Former Courthouse for James City County and the City of Williamsburg

Designed in the manner of the eighteenth century, this modern building served as the courthouse for the city of Williamsburg and James City County from 1932 until 1968. Plans call for the removal of this building and the reconstruction of the large frame house, with numerous outbuildings, built here by Robert Carter Nicholas. Nicholas, treasurer of the colony and later a chancery court

judge, bought the property in 1770. Among the subsequent owners was John Tyler, tenth president of the United States. Tyler, as the newly elected vice-president, was living here in 1841 when word reached Williamsburg that President William Henry Harrison had died.

Nicholas-Tyler Laundry—S.

The original of this typical small building was described in an insur-

ance policy of 1801, at which time it was valued at $100. Old photographs further assisted the architects in the reconstruction. Used first as a kitchen, then as a laundry, it is now privately occupied.

FRANCIS STREET BECOMES
FRANCE STREET

In the eighteenth century, at this point, the steep sides and muddy bottom of a ravine severed Francis Street on the east from France Street to the west. Today they form a thoroughfare, with only a dip and curve to mark the end of one and the beginning of the other.

Custis Kitchen—S.

Standing alone on what was once part of Eastern State Hospital grounds is an early nineteenth-century kitchen. It marks property that was owned by Colonel John Custis—scholar, planter, and eccentric—and subsequently known as Custis Square. Here Custis built a brick residence and cultivated his celebrated garden, vestiges of which still remained at the time of the Civil War. Correspondence recording his exchange of plant specimens with the great English natural history enthusiast, Peter Collinson, has been helpful in planting the gardens of Williamsburg. When Custis died in 1749, the property passed to his son, Daniel Parke Custis, whose widow subsequently married George Washington. Washington administered the property until his stepson, John Parke Custis, came of age in 1778, at which time Custis Square was sold at auction. Colonial Williamsburg now owns the property and looks forward to the time when Mr. Custis's garden and his "Six Chimney House," as it was called, can be reestablished there.

INTERSECTION OF
NASSAU STREET

Site of Eastern State Hospital—S.

Founded in 1770 and long known as the "Lunatick Hospital," this was the earliest state-owned hospital in North America devoted entirely to mental illness. In colonial times the care of the insane, like the care of paupers, was considered a local matter and usually was left to the vestry of the parish. The vestry was unable to finance or maintain an asylum, and hence the insane were either left at large in a world with which they could not cope or were placed in prison where they were often badly mistreated. Realizing this, the humane Governor Francis Fauquier directed the attention of the burgesses to the need for better care for "persons who are so unhappy as to be deprived of their reason," and an act was passed in 1770 "to make Provision for the support and maintenance of ideots, lunatics, and other persons of unsound Minds." The hospital, designed by a well-known Philadelphia architect, Robert Smith, was opened in 1773. Among its original trustees were Peyton Randolph, George Wythe, Thomas Nelson "The Signer," John Blair, John Tazewell, and John Randolph "The Tory." Disastrous fires swept the hospital in 1876 and 1885, the latter razing all the principal colonial buildings. Today the hospital has about 1,700 patients and a staff of over 1,000, all of whom have been transferred to extensive new facilities on the western outskirts of Williamsburg. In due time a reconstruction of the eighteenth-century hospital building will be undertaken, based on archaeological and historical research as well as on the original architectural drawings.

Travis House—N.

Through the middle years of the eighteenth century the property here belonged by bequest to Bruton Parish. The vestry of the church, in order to sell the lots, had to have permission of the colonial government —in the form of an act passed by the General Assembly, signed by the governor, and approved by the king. The purchaser built the first section of this long narrow house in about 1763, well before the legal red tape had been unwound. He was Colonel Edward Champion Travis, a member of the House of Burgesses representing the "rotten borough" of Jamestown. Subjected to a complicated sequence of modifications and enlargements, the house at one time was the residence of the superintendent of Eastern State Hospital. It stood on its present location until 1929, was twice moved, and in 1968 was returned to its original site. Like the twentieth-century brick building close behind it, the restored Travis House is privately occupied.

INTERSECTION OF HENRY STREET

Griffin House—S.

Unrestored. Built about 1769, this house was owned by Samuel Griffin, a Revolutionary officer who became a member of the Continental Congress. Griffin married the daughter of Carter Braxton, one of the Virginia signers of the Declaration of Independence. Privately occupied.

Nicholson Street—East to West

Coke-Garrett House—N.

The five lots occupied by this restored house, its outbuildings, and its garden, had a checkered record of ownership through the first half of the eighteenth century. Finally in 1755 John Coke, who already owned the three easternmost lots, added the two nearest the Gaol; the property has been a unit ever since. Coke, a successful goldsmith and tavern-keeper, left a personal estate valued at £772 when he died in 1767. His widow, Sarah, continued to operate or rent out the house as a tavern. In 1777 she had to petition the House of

Delegates to compensate her for damage done by Continental troops quartered here. Her versatile son Robey, who lived with his mother, repaired wagons, mounted cannon, helved axes, and made rammers for Revolutionary militiamen. The property was acquired by the Garrett family of Williamsburg about 1810 and remained in its possession for well over a century.

During that time a great many structural changes took place. The present house is actually composed of three distinct structures. The western section was standing here when John Coke bought it in 1755, and the eastern wing is also of eighteenth-century vintage, but was moved here shortly after 1837, when the central part was built. The subdued Greek Revival architecture of this center section merges easily with the colonial styles of the wings. The detached office, dating from early in the nineteenth century, bears full evidence of the Greek Revival fashion in its columned and pedimented porch.

The garden west of the house is largely evergreen; various sections are separated by hedges of dwarf box. Pasture serves as a transition at the edge of town. The small family graveyard at the rear was a common feature in parts of Virginia. Privately occupied.

THE PUBLIC GAOL

On the northern side of Nicholson Street stands the Public Gaol, referred to by a reliable eighteenth-century chronicler as a "strong sweet Prison." After 250 years it remains today grim evidence of crime and punishment in colonial America. Now restored, it is an exhibition building of Colonial Williamsburg. Both common criminals awaiting summary justice and debtors awaiting succor or mercy were confined here. The imprisonment of debtors, however, was practically eliminated after 1772 as the result of an act making creditors wholly responsible for the maintenance of debtors and trebling the fees for their board. The General Court, which met twice a year at the Capitol, tried offenses punishable by mutilation or death. Lesser offenders were forced to undergo the discomfort and public ridicule of the pillory or stocks, barbarous but effective instruments of justice which today's visitors may try without the inconvenience of a padlock.

Henry Cary, the master builder who supervised construction of both Capitol and Palace, was ordered by the Assembly to begin work in 1701 on a "Publick Gaol" (pronounced "jail" as today). By 1704 the Gaol was ready to receive its first guests. Debtors' cells were added in 1711. Keeper's quarters were built in 1722, the period to which the building has been restored. The Gaol served colony and commonwealth until 1780, and thereafter a portion of the original building continued to be used by the city of Williamsburg as its jail until 1910. In 1933 it was deeded to Colonial Williamsburg by the city. Part of the brickwork of its massive walls is original and some of the early interior finish was found. In the course of excavations, shackles were unearthed, evidence of the bleak life of an unlucky few.

Although frequently tempered with mercy, the treatment and disposition of criminals in the Virginia colony seems inhumane in the light of prison reforms of the past two centuries. Yet it should be recalled that colonial society included not only the usual lawless elements but newly arrived slaves, transported convicts, runaway indentured servants, pirates, and marauding Indians. It was a society not far removed from the frontier, one in which hot tempers, high spirits, and little education often produced crimes of the worst sort. Furthermore, it was costly to build and maintain prisons so that it was customary to clear criminal cells of their inmates after each session of the General Court. Thus, with the exception of debtors, persons convicted by this court were usually fined, lashed, branded, mutilated, or hanged. Debtors who could not gain relief through friends or family were forced to await the ultimate mercy of the court.

Yet despite leg irons, handcuffs, and chains, despite bitter cold nights spent on floor matting of malodorous straw, and despite a diet of "salt beef damaged, and Indian meal," the life of the prisoners was not wholly without mitigation. During daylight hours they were often allowed to walk about and converse in the exercise yard. Sanitary arrangements, although crude, were advanced for that century. In cases of illness, "Physick" was provided, and more fortunate prisoners were permitted to return to their homes until recovery. Those with an adequate purse could buy meals or liquor from one of the taverns in the vicinity and often shared these luxuries with others. A group of Indians, thrown into the unheated cells in the winter of 1704-1705, was provided with greatcoats by the Assembly. One keeper, in advertising the detention of a runaway slave, urged his owner to "make as speedily application for him as possible that he may not suffer from the inclemency of the season."

A prisoner sentenced to death was allowed several weeks to make his peace with God, and during this period was brought each Sunday to Bruton Parish Church by the gaoler. The death penalty was inflicted for many offenses, including arson, piracy, horse stealing, forgery, and burglary. Cases were carefully weighed, however, and clemency sometimes offered first offenders or criminals with a particularly moving plea. In 1718 fifteen henchmen of the pirate Blackbeard were imprisoned in the Gaol, and thirteen of them were subsequently hanged; yet in 1727,

John Vidal, a convicted pirate who pitifully protested that he "never intended to go a-pirating" and who "with a weeping heart" prayed for a longer time for repentance, was granted His Majesty's most gracious pardon.

The Gaol also served at times as a madhouse and a military prison. The mentally ill were often confined here until the erection of the "Lunatick Hospital," now Eastern State Hospital. During the turbulent early years of the Revolution, the Gaol was badly overcrowded with British redcoats, Tory sympathizers, traitors, deserters, and spies. Gaol fever broke out among them and many died, although the fever was controlled somewhat by cleaning the vaults and washing the floors with vinegar and sprinkling them with wild mint. The most famous prisoner during this period was Henry Hamilton, the British governor of the Northwest Territory, widely known as the "Hair Buyer" because he was believed to pay his Indian allies for American scalps.

The keeper's quarters are furnished with simple, serviceable pieces. Gaolkeepers were paid little, and had a rough and dangerous job. The first keeper, John Redwood, received only £30 annually. Despite increased pay, each of his twelve colonial successors complained that his income was inadequate to the hazards of the office. One gaoler, "knock'd down" by a quart bottle in the hand of an escaping murderer, was discharged for his pains.

The best-known keeper was the erudite Peter Pelham, organist at Boston's Trinity Church before taking up the same post at Bruton Parish Church in 1755. He augmented his income by providing music for Williamsburg's second theater and by teaching young ladies to master the harpsichord and spinet. Pelham was musical director when

The Begger's Opera was first performed in Williamsburg. He became also, in 1771, the keeper of the Gaol. There were some who suggested that Pelham further increased his income by permitting convicted prisoners to escape. However, he was cleared of all charges against him in an inquiry ordered by the Assembly.

William Randolph Lodging—S.

This unusually narrow building, reconstructed at the rear of the Russell lot, was "letten for Lodgins" in 1735 to William Randolph of Turkey Island, burgess and later councillor. His younger brother, Sir John Randolph, was Peyton's father.

INTERSECTION OF
BOTETOURT STREET

Elizabeth Reynolds House—S.

Now reconstructed, a small, narrow, two-story frame dwelling was erected here about 1777 by William Hunter, Jr., a proprietor of the *Virginia Gazette,* for Elizabeth Reynolds, his mother. Hunter, a "natural son" of Elizabeth Reynolds, deeded this strip of land behind the *Gazette* office to his mother "in consideration of the natural love and Affection which he hath." Together with house and property, he also deeded her an annuity of £40 and furnished a "servant maid fit and able to serve wait and attend" her. Privately occupied.

Anthony Hay's Cabinetmaking Shop—N.

Anthony Hay had been a Williamsburg cabinetmaker for at least five years when he bought this property in 1756. He probably built the shop immediately thereafter, partly astraddle the small stream at the bottom of the ravine. After he became keeper of the Raleigh Tavern in 1767, Hay's shop was leased to a series of cabinetmakers, including Benjamin Bucktrout and Edmund Dickinson. His family occupied a house on adjoining lots, and his

widow continued to hold the property after Hay died in 1770.

Two operating craft shops in the Colonial Williamsburg program share this reconstructed building today. In the larger part a cabinetmaker carries on the ancient skill of making fine furniture by hand, using the cabinet woods of eighteenth-century Virginia —cherry, walnut, and imported mahogany—and the tools of that period. Among the latter, the foot- and hand-powered lathes are of particular interest. In the smaller wing a maker of musical instruments plies his own meticulous craft of fashioning harpsichords, "guittars," and other instruments known from newspaper advertisements to have been made here.

INTERSECTION OF
COLONIAL STREET

Tayloe House—N.

Built midway in the eighteenth century, this gambrel-roofed dwelling changed hands in 1759 for £600— a very high price for a frame house at that time. It was purchased as a town house by one of the wealthiest colonial Virginians, Colonel John Tayloe, owner of the magnificent

plantation Mount Airy on the Northern Neck. Tayloe served as justice of the peace as soon as he came of age, and was later for many years a member of the Council. Although a firm supporter of the rights of the colonies and a warm friend of Washington, Tayloe could not reconcile himself to complete separation from Great Britain, and declined to serve when elected a member of the new commonwealth's council in 1776. He preferred to retire from public life. The office, just east of the restored house, has an interesting bell-shaped roof. Privately occupied.

INTERSECTION OF
QUEEN STREET

Ludwell Tenement—N.

At the division of the Ludwell estate in 1770 this property was described as "the Tenement adjoining the Speaker," meaning the rental property next to the home of Peyton Randolph. Randolph's nephew, Harrison Randolph, lived here in 1779. An old resident of Williamsburg remembered how the building looked before the Civil War, when it was destroyed. Reconstructed; Privately occupied.

PEYTON RANDOLPH HOUSE

PEYTON RANDOLPH, one of the leading statesmen of colonial America, served as speaker of the House of Burgesses from 1766 until 1775. He was known as a conservative, yet he took the patriot side in the struggle with England and was chosen president of the First Continental Congress in Philadelphia in 1774.

Sir John Randolph, Peyton's father, was the most distinguished lawyer in Virginia in the first third of the eighteenth century. Educated at William and Mary and the Inns of Court, he was clerk of the House of Burgesses in 1728 when that body sent him to London as its special agent. During a second similar assignment he was knighted, the only colonial Virginian to be so honored. In 1734 he was elected to represent the College of William and Mary

in the House of Burgesses, and that body at once chose him as its speaker.

Sir John, who died in 1737, willed the house to his wife for her lifetime, and after that to his second son, Peyton. Sir John also left his library to Peyton, who was about sixteen when his father died, "hoping he will betake himself to the study of law." After Peyton Randolph died in 1775, Thomas Jefferson bought the library. Jefferson's library in turn became the nucleus of the Library of Congress, and a number of Randolph's books have been identified by signature or bookplate among the Jefferson collection there.

Peyton Randolph followed his father's advice and studied law in London after attending William and Mary. He was appointed attorney general of the colony of Virginia in

1744 and was elected to the House of Burgesses in 1748. In 1753 the burgesses chose him to go to London to present their protest against Governor Dinwiddie's pistole fee. Elected speaker of the House in 1766, he presided over it at every session in the crucial decade before the Revolution. It was to his experience as speaker that Thomas Lynch of South Carolina referred when he nominated Randolph to be president of the First Continental Congress. His unanimous election showed the confidence that the other delegates had in him.

The preceding July 13, Randolph's constituents in Williamsburg had demonstrated their admiration for him by reversing the custom of the candidate's treating the voters: the freeholders of Williamsburg had a dinner for their burgess at the Raleigh Tavern. Afterward they accompanied him back to his house, where they gave him three cheers and wished him long life.

There was another gathering at the Peyton Randolph House that summer that had greater political significance. In August, just before the Continental Congress convened, legislators were meeting in Williamsburg to determine the course of Virginia's delegates to the Congress. Thomas Jefferson, lying ill upcountry, was unable to reach Williamsburg but sent his suggestions to his cousin, Peyton Randolph, and they were read aloud here to a group of the patriots. Jefferson's document was soon printed as *A Summary View of the Rights of British America*. Too radical for some but moving to all, it was among the most influential tracts along the road to independence.

Mrs. Betty Harrison Randolph continued to live in the house after her husband's death. She relinquished it for a time during the Revolution when the comte de Rochambeau set up headquarters here before the Yorktown campaign, at the same time that Washington occupied the George Wythe House. Mrs. Mary Monroe Peachy was living here in 1824 when she offered her house to General Lafayette on his visit in October. Welcomed by the mayor, Lafayette in turn addressed the assembled crowd.

Although Peyton Randolph may have been born in Williamsburg about 1721, it cannot be said with certainty that he was born in the house that now bears his name. Sir John Randolph and his family were living in the westernmost section of the house (built about 1715) in 1724. In that year he bought the lot and the one-and-one-half story house next door. Sometime thereafter the two houses were linked by the middle two-story section. Colonial Williamsburg acquired the house in 1938 and restored it in 1940, reconstructing the east wing at that time. The former owner and life tenant now lives in that wing, graciously allowing the original portion to be shown as an exhibition building.

Noteworthy features of the restored part of the house are the wooden belt board at the second-floor line and the hooded front entrance. Inside the house is the best series of original paneled rooms in Williamsburg. Most of the paneling is the usual yellow pine, but the northeast room on the second floor of the oldest section is paneled completely in oak.

Robertson's Windmill—N.

In the area behind the Peyton Randolph House stood one of the most familiar landmarks of any colonial scene—a windmill. Late in the eighteenth century, milling developed into a large-scale industry in Virginia as wheat became a second staple along with tobacco. The colonial householder could either buy meal or flour for "ready money" or—if he brought his own grain—could barter or else allow the miller to exact his time-honored percentage—his "toll." In Virginia, white cornmeal was a prime favorite. The miller would have had one or more assistants to keep the mill facing the wind and to manage the grinding and sacking operation. In a high wind, the miller had to turn mariner and furl his canvas sails, which were tightly lashed top and bottom to the lattice frames of the four wide arms of the mill.

Two types of windmills were common in the colonial period: a tower mill, a fixed structure of which only the hooded top moved; and a post mill, the earliest form of mill known, which appeared in Europe during the Middle Ages. The post mill was so

called because the whole superstructure revolved on top of a single huge post of hewn timber. The superstructure had two levels—the upper chamber held the main shaft and millstones, and the lower chamber held the screening and sacking machinery.

Robertson's Windmill is the post type, which was well known on the peninsula and had the advantage of having no fixed foundations so that it could be hauled to a new location.

William Robertson, the first known owner of the mill, was clerk of the Council from 1698 until his death in 1739. In 1723 he sold four lots, including houses and the windmill, to John Holloway for the reasonable sum of £80. Today Robertson's Windmill is an operating Colonial Williamsburg craft shop.

INTERSECTION OF
NORTH ENGLAND STREET

Archibald Blair House—N.

This property was acquired in 1716 by Dr. Archibald Blair. The frame

later it was recovered by Archibald's son John, and eventually passed to his son, Dr. James Blair, a physician. During the Revolution it was occupied for six years by James Madison, president of the College of William and Mary and later first Episcopal bishop of Virginia. Privately occupied.

St. George Tucker House—N.

One of Williamsburg's most admired houses, this restored residence is marked by its repeating gabled roofs of various sizes, its widely spaced dormer windows, and its massive chimneys. Because of its narrow width, the second story has excellent light and ventilation, but requires five stairways. The earliest owner of the house was the noted jurist St. George Tucker, and it has continued in the possession of this family ever since. Tucker, who became known as the "American Blackstone" because of his annotated edition of the celebrated *Commentaries*, published in 1803, purchased the property in 1788. He moved an older building—believed to be the Levingston House—to this site and enlarged it by several additions. The Levingston House had faced on Palace Green, but when the capital moved to Richmond and the Palace burned down, the focus of city life shifted to the Courthouse and Market Square. The lawyer, naturally, preferred to face his house toward the center of town. Tucker, a native of Bermuda, attended the College of William and Mary and was active in the cause of

house, a full two stories with no dormers in the roof, was erected in mid-century. It has now been restored. On each floor are two rooms, each with a generous corner fireplace, on either side of a central hall. Although the front porch is later in date than the house, it was retained because of its architectural appeal.

Dr. Blair was a Scottish physician who emigrated to Virginia in 1690, perhaps because of the position and influence of his brother, Reverend James Blair, at that time commissary in Virginia of the bishop of London and subsequently founder and first president of the College of William and Mary. Archibald Blair supplemented the practice of medicine with the pursuits of commerce and conducted a business described by Governor Spotswood in 1718 as "one of the most considerable Trading Stores in this Country." Blair was for many years a vestryman of Bruton Parish Church and a burgess for Jamestown. He died in 1733, and the house later became the property of John Randolph "The Tory," who sold it to Dr. Peter Hay in 1763. Eight years

the colonies during the Revolution. He was appointed judge of the Virginia General Court in 1788, and federal district judge in 1813; in 1790 he succeeded George Wythe as professor of law at the College.

The house, which is privately occupied, has been painted in colors specified in an agreement made between Tucker and a local painter and confirmed by surface scrapings made in the twentieth century.

Palace Green—East Side

Levingston Kitchen—E.

The original building on this site was a dependency of the house of William Levingston, who built his theater on the adjacent lot. The smaller building remained for some time after the house itself had been removed, possibly to become part of the St. George Tucker House. The massive chimney and the heavy cornice overhang, which provides added room on the second floor, give the reconstructed kitchen architectural distinction. Privately occupied.

Site of the First Theater—E.

Archaeologists unearthed here the foundations of the first theater to be established in English America. Measurements prove the building to have been 30 feet wide by 86½ feet long. This is not, however, conspicuously small in comparison with English provincial theaters of the period.

William Levingston, a merchant from New Kent County, moved to Williamsburg and erected the theater about 1716. In *The Present State of Virginia,* a book published in England in 1724, Reverend Hugh Jones referred to it as "a Play House and a good Bowling Green." In spite of his auspicious start, impresario Levingston suffered financial reverses and was forced to mortgage the property in 1721 and to give up the theater and leave Williamsburg in 1727. However, the building continued to be used periodically; in the autumn of 1736 *The Tragedy of Cato* was performed here by "the young Gentlemen of the College," and *The Busy-Body, The Recruiting Officer,* and *The Beaux' Stratagem* by "the Gentlemen and Ladies of this Country." In 1745 the old playhouse was purchased for £50 by a group of subscribers and was given to the city of Williamsburg to be used as a municipal court and city hall. Repaired and reshingled, it served as the hustings court until 1770, when it was razed.

BRUSH-EVERARD HOUSE

ON THE east side of Palace Green stands the restored Brush-Everard House, one of the exhibition buildings of Colonial Williamsburg. This frame building, once known to readers of Mary Johnston's popular novel *Audrey* as the home of the heroine, was built in 1717 by John Brush, gunsmith, armorer, and first keeper of the colony's Magazine on Market Square. Apparently the building served him as both shop and residence. William Dering, teacher of dancing at the College, bought the property in 1742. His importance in the social life of Williamsburg is indicated by his announcements in the *Virginia Gazette* of 1745 and 1746 that, as one advertisement put it, "for the Entertainment of Gentlemen and Ladies, there will be Balls and Assemblies at the Capitol, every other

Night, during the Court, by their humble Servant, *William Dering*." Dering was also an artist, and his inventory listed a large number of pictures and "one paint box." One painting now hanging in the parlor bears his signature.

The house eventually came into the hands of Thomas Everard, who was clerk of York County from 1745 until his death twenty-six years later. He also served as auditor of Virginia and clerk of the General Court. In 1766 and again in 1771 he was elected mayor of Williamsburg and undoubtedly lived in the city at those times. A man of comfortable circumstances, although not wealthy, Everard is believed to have enlarged the house and embellished the interior. The addition of two wings at the rear resulted in a U-shaped plan, of which

Williamsburg has one other example in the Elkanah Deane House. The staircase in the house is remarkably fine, with elaborately turned balusters and sweeping hand rails. The stair brackets are richly ornamented with original carving almost identical in design and execution to the famous staircases at Carter's Grove in James City County and Tuckahoe in Goochland County. The first floor front rooms and central hall have paneled wainscoting. In two other rooms there is wallpaper that reproduces the design of fragments found in the house.

The yard between the house and the outbuildings is paved with the original brick disclosed in the course of excavations. The brick kitchen and the wooden smokehouse are original buildings that have been restored. Turf panels run back to the lot line as it existed when Brush owned the property. Later the garden was enlarged and a small pond was added—an unusual feature in colonial Williamsburg. Today the ancient box claims first attention. Dwarf box, originally forming a hedge on each side of the axial garden walk, has grown in 150 years into a mass of tall twisted trees, now among the oldest surviving box in Williamsburg.

Everard was a gentleman of standing in the community, although less celebrated than George Wythe and other prominent Virginians who were his friends. The Brush-Everard House represents a town house somewhat more modest than the Wythe House nearby, and the furnishings, including many examples of southern colonial furniture, have been chosen accordingly.

It is more difficult to depict the furnishing of a man's mind, but a library has been assembled in the house based upon a list compiled by Thomas Jefferson in 1771 for the guidance of a well-to-do planter of average intellectual interests. Consisting of about 300 volumes, this library shows in tangible form an important element in the cultural life of colonial Virginia. The titles are distributed among the classics, drama, history, law, philosophy, religion, and science. In a letter explaining his selection, Jefferson rejected the notion that "nothing can be useful but the learned lumber of Greek and Roman reading," and maintained that "a little attention . . . to the nature of the human mind evinces that the entertainments of fiction are useful as well as pleasant." Jefferson calculated the cost of this library at about £100 sterling in plain bindings, and half as much again in fine marbled bindings. A pamphlet describing the library is available at the Prentis Store.

THE GOVERNOR'S PALACE

RECONSTRUCTED on its old foundations, the Palace—symbol of the power and prestige of the crown in colonial Virginia—stands once more in a commanding position at the northern end of Palace Green. It is an exhibition building of Colonial Williamsburg. This was the official residence of seven royal governors, from Alexander Spotswood, who supervised its building, to Lord Dunmore, who fled from it before dawn one June morning in 1775, thus ending for all time British rule in Virginia. When the new commonwealth came into being, the Palace served as the executive mansion for the first two governors, Patrick Henry and Thomas Jefferson.

In 1706, a few years after the capital of the colony had been moved to Williamsburg from Jamestown, the Assembly was prevailed upon to set aside £3,000 for the erection of an official mansion for the governors. Henry Cary, the master builder who supervised the construction of the Capitol, was placed in charge, and Alexander Spotswood, governor from 1710 to 1722, devoted his personal attention to the project.

The building was not formally completed until about 1720, by which time it had earned the sobriquet of "Palace" from colonists who resented the additional levies required for its construction.

The Palace, including the buildings that surround it, is admirably adapted to express its dual function as a residence and as the official headquarters of the king's deputy in a great agricultural colony. The main building is usually described as Georgian in style, and in many respects resembles English country estates of the period of the first two Georges. The official character of the Palace is suggested in the playfully fortified effect created by the castellated walls in the forecourt, and is emphasized in the stately cupola (or lantern) rising above the balustraded roof. For special occasions the lantern was brilliantly illuminated. Dutch influence, introduced into England by William III, is discernible in this and in other features. The Renaissance is reflected in the formal gardens and the orderly layout of the flanking buildings and other dependencies. But the broad chimneys of the outbuildings and the characteristic shapes of smokehouse, laundry, wellhead, and salthouse lend a distinctly Virginia flavor, suggesting a plantation on the outskirts of town. In its unification of many converging influences, the Palace bears the unmistakable stamp of Virginia plantation architecture; it could have been built only in the colonial South.

In 1751 extensive repair work was authorized and the interior is believed to have been remodeled. It was probably at this time that a wing was added to provide a ballroom and supper room adequate for the official entertaining required of the royal representative. An invitation to the Palace was a distinction and might well serve a political purpose as well as the personal pleasure of the governor and his lady. In 1769 Lord Botetourt mentioned in a letter, "Fifty two dined with me yesterday, and I expect at least that number today." Food was carried to the formal dining room in great covered containers from the service area west of the building. Of course entertainment was costly; Governor Gooch ruefully noted that a celebration at a royal "Birth-Night" drew 100 guineas from his own purse. Along with the expense of servants and food, the "Binn Cellar," with hundreds of gallons of imported wines, had to be replenished.

The upper middle room recalls the more initimate side of Palace life. Here the governor could be at ease with a few friends or could peruse the latest volume to arrive from England. After long search, appropriate editions of most of the books listed in Governor Botetourt's library have been assembled in this pleasant room. The east flanking building is furnished as the governor's office; the opposite flanking building is furnished as a guardhouse.

In the gardens, yet another story was revealed: in the course of excavations for the reconstruction, twentieth-century investigators unearthed tragic evidence of patriot troops who died while the Palace was serving as a military hospital during the Yorktown campaign. In eleven orderly rows were discovered the unmarked graves of 156 Revolutionary veterans and two women thought to have been nurses. Today a simple stone tablet commemorates their sacrifice and the branches of a weeping willow shade the plot.

At the Palace, as in the less pretentious gardens of Williamsburg, the formality of English design is seen. Here we find elaborate geometrical parterres, framed with clipped hedges and accented with topiary work. Pleached allées offer shade, and the plain parterre of the tree-box garden affords a green for a game of bowls. Standing watch over the garden are twelve yaupons, a fast-growing holly native to this area. "Twelve apostles" have been found on English estates of the period. Additional "conceits" add to the pleasure of visitors. One such is the holly maze, patterned after the maze at Hampton Court; it is overlooked by a lofty, tree-shaded mount built to insulate the icehouse. The fishpond and terraced gardens to the west of the Palace were apparently controversial features to budget-minded legislators, for Governor Spotswood in 1718 offered "if the Assembly did not care to be at the Expense of the Fish-Pond and Falling Gardens, to take them to my Self." The colony provided "standing furniture" for the Palace but most of the furnishings were the personal property of the governor, imported by him from England or purchased from his predecessor. When a gover-

nor died in Virginia, a careful accounting was rendered, and it has been from these inventories that the reconstructed building has been furnished. Virtually all furnishings of the Palace are antiques that have been acquired for the most part in England.

Reconstruction of the Palace, destroyed by fire in 1781, was begun in 1930. Excavations disclosed the original basement walls largely intact and foundations of many dependencies. Research workers were aided by the floor plan drawn by Thomas Jefferson in 1779, by the Bodleian Plate, and by the Frenchman's Map, all described earlier. Further significant information about the Palace was found in the journals of the House of Burgesses and in other colonial records.

Palace Green — West Side

Robert Carter House—W.

This stately old house was built sometime before 1746. For a time in 1751–1752, while the Palace was undergoing repairs, it served as the residence of Governor Dinwiddie. The first known owner was Charles Carter, son of Robert "King" Carter. He sold the property in 1746, but in 1753 it was purchased by another member of the family, Robert Carter Nicholas, long a leader of the conservative faction of the House of Burgesses and treasurer of the colony. Nicholas made it his home until 1761, when he sold it to his cousin, Councillor Robert Carter of Nomini Hall. Carter was a true product of the eighteenth-century enlightenment—a cultivated gentleman, a liberal, and a patriot. He lived in the house for twelve years and here entertained many distinguished persons including, on more than one occasion, George Washington. Of the seventeen Carter children, six were born here. Finding the house understandably "not sufficiently roomy," the Carters withdrew in 1772 to the plantation life described in the journal of the children's tutor, Philip Fithian. In 1801 the Williamsburg property was sold to Robert Saunders, who bequeathed it to his son Robert, fourteenth president of the College. Like the house, the brick outbuilding is original; other dependencies—including the unusual "breezeway"—were reconstructed from documentary records. The contorted tree that stands before the house is a paper mulberry, age unknown. The house and its northern dependency are privately occupied.

McKenzie Apothecary Shop—W.

Open as a craft exhibition during the busy season, this shop displays the herb jars and tincture bottles of a colonial doctor and druggist. Dr. Kenneth McKenzie owned such a shop in Williamsburg from 1732 until his death in 1755. The atmosphere and activity here are essentially the same as in the Pasteur-Galt Apothecary Shop on Duke of Gloucester Street.

Elkanah Deane House—W.

The original dwelling on this site was purchased by Elkanah Deane, an Irish coachmaker, who paid £700 for the house, shop, and garden in 1772. Deane may have been encouraged to move to Williamsburg be-

cause, while working in New York, he was ordered to make a coach, phaeton, and chaise for Governor Dunmore. Although described by one disgruntled rival in the *Gazette* as "an Hibernian Cottager" and the "Palace Street Puffer," Deane earned a name for himself making and repairing all kinds of carriages, harness, steel springs, and ironwork, as well as painting, gilding, and japanning. He died in 1775.

The house itself disappeared soon after 1800 and has been reconstructed. The back porch looks out over a geometric garden, open to the public, in which the tree-box topiary and regular planting of small-leaved lindens are conspicuous features. Privately occupied.

INTERSECTION OF PRINCE GEORGE STREET

GEORGE WYTHE HOUSE

IN THIS solid brick mansion on the west side of Palace Green, now restored as one of the exhibition buildings of Colonial Williamsburg, lived George Wythe, a mild-mannered, soft-spoken man who was one of the most influential Americans of his era. Wythe (pronounced to rhyme with Smith) was a product of Virginia's plantation society. He was born in 1726 in Elizabeth City County where his father, who died soon after, was a successful planter. Wythe attended school at William and Mary for a brief time and, encouraged by his mother, read widely in the classics, a custom frequently followed by cultured members of the gentry. He be-

came perhaps the foremost classical scholar in Virginia. After studying law for a short time, he was admitted to the bar at the age of twenty. For a few years he practiced law in Spotsylvania, in partnership with John Lewis. In 1747 he married Lewis's sister Ann, but within a year of the ceremony death claimed his young bride.

Williamsburg had become Wythe's home by 1754, for in that year he was elected to represent the city as a burgess. At this time he also acted as the colony's attorney general while his friend Peyton Randolph was on a mission in England. It was also about this time that he married Elizabeth Taliaferro (pronounced Tolli-ver), daughter of Colonel Richard Taliaferro, who is believed to have designed and built the Wythe House for his daughter and son-in-law. Their only child died in infancy.

The public career of George Wythe spanned a decisive half-century in American life: as executor and close friend of the popular royal governors Fauquier and Botetourt, he saw the power of the crown at its peak; as a burgess during most of the years from 1754 to 1769, and clerk of the House from 1769 to 1775, he sided with the patriots in the growing dispute with Parliament; as a legislator and justice during the formation of the young republic, he fought for independence, the protection of individual liberties, and the authority of the courts. He ably supported Richard Henry Lee's resolution for independence at Philadelphia, and his name appears first among Virginia signers of the Declaration of Independence. He counseled Virginia to establish a regular army instead of a militia, and himself volunteered for service, but he was chosen instead to become speaker of the House of Delegates in 1777, and, in 1778, one of the three judges of Virginia's High Court of Chancery. Working with Jefferson and Edmund Pendleton, he aided in revising the laws of Virginia.

This distinguished record was, however, fully matched in importance by Wythe's influence as a teacher and adviser. He probably did more to shape Jefferson's ideas than any other man. Wythe first knew the future president as a thoughtful, freckle-faced student at the College of William and Mary. Later Jefferson studied law in Wythe's office, and referred to him as "my faithful and beloved Mentor in youth, and my most affectionate friend through life." The Jefferson family stayed at the Wythe House for several weeks in 1776.

In 1779 Wythe was appointed to the newly established chair of law at William and Mary and thus became the first professor of law in an American college. Among his students was John Marshall, later chief justice of the United States. Wythe resigned his professorship after a decade and, having been appointed sole judge of the Court of Chancery, moved to Richmond. There his brilliant career ended tragically in 1806. He was poisoned, probably by George Sweeney, a grandnephew who lived with him. Sweeney, in desperate financial straits, had hoped to profit as the principal beneficiary under his uncle's will. The aged statesman lived in agony for two weeks, long enough to disinherit his grandnephew. Sweeney was never convicted, however, largely because the testimony of a slave who witnessed the act was not then admissible in Virginia courts. Like many Virginians of his time, Wythe opposed slavery in principle and freed his servants in his will. To Jefferson—then president—he bequeathed his "books and small philosophical apparatus," and his "silver cups and goldheaded cane." He is buried in St. John's Churchyard, Richmond.

The Wythe House served as headquarters for Washington just before the siege of Yorktown, and for Rochambeau after the surrender of Cornwallis. It passed through the hands of many owners, and in 1926 was purchased by interested individuals and organizations and given to Bruton Parish Church to be used as a parish house. Some restoration work was undertaken at that time. After 1938, when it was acquired by Colonial Williamsburg, restoration of the building and grounds was completed.

A large kitchen garden provided produce for the family table and fowl were kept in the chicken house. Other provisions brought from the country were stored in the smokehouse and elsewhere. Typical in plan, the mansion is spacious but simple. Two rooms on each side flank the large central hall on both the first and second stories. Two great chimneys rise between the paired rooms, thus affording a fireplace in all eight. The smaller windows in the second story have the same number of panes as those on the first floor, a device that adds to the apparent scale of the house. Horizontal brick lines at the water table and at the belt course between the first and second floors relieve the severe lines of the exterior.

Furnishings include both English and American pieces. No inventory has been discovered, although a few orders sent by Wythe to England were found; the house, therefore, has been refurnished with the guidance of inventories of similar houses owned by men of comparable wealth and background. Worthy of particular note are the two back rooms on the first floor, one furnished as Mr. Wythe's study and the other as a student's room with an asemblage of the kind of scientific apparatus that Wythe might have had.

Behind the house extends a pleasure garden lined with tree-box topiary and terminating in a pleached arbor of hornbeam. House, outbuildings, and gardens form zones of use. Brick and marl paths link the service area, kitchen garden, and herb garden with the main house.

Wythe South Office—W

One of Colonial Williamsburg's operating craft shops, the basketmaker is housed in a reconstructed

outbuilding of the Wythe House. Like barrels, baskets were used in many shapes and sizes for storing and carrying all manner of things. Split oak is the material employed in this craft demonstration.

Prince George Street—East to West

Deane Forge and Harness-making Shop—N.

Reconstructed. The onetime workshop of coachmaker Elkanah Deane today houses two of Colonial Williamsburg's operating craft shops.

Using the simple tools of the eighteenth century, the blacksmith fashions and repairs all kinds of ironware. Every farm and home in the neighborhood needed many of the hardware items—from wagon tires to smoothing irons—that he produced.

In Williamsburg the farrier's trade —the shoeing of horses—was but a minor facet of the blacksmith's work. The soil of tidewater Virginia being sandy and free of stones, horses usually went unshod.

The saddler and harnessmaker, on the contrary, was a busy man. Every Virginian, it seemed, owned a horse and rode it constantly. And every burden transported by land had to be lifted and hauled by horse, oxen, or slave power. Hence the maker of harness and saddles was vitally important to the comfort and economy of the community, and he was likely to be correspondingly prosperous.

Matthew Whaley School—N.

North of the intersection of Nassau Street stands a modern building that houses one of Williamsburg's older institutions. The Matthew Whaley School, a public elementary school, is named in memory of a nine-year-old boy who died in 1705. His widowed mother bequeathed more than £500 to "eternalize" her son through a "free school."

Timson House.

On the northwest corner of Prince George and Nassau Streets is one of the oldest houses in Williamsburg, built before 1717. It is privately occupied and has not been restored.

South England Street—North to South

Lightfoot Tenement—E.

A rental property in the eighteenth century. Now a guesthouse for Williamsburg Inn. See page 65.

Former Courthouse for James City County and the City of Williamsburg—W.

See page 65.

Craft House—E.

Reproductions of many Williamsburg antiques are on sale at Craft House. These reproductions include furniture, glass, silver, brass, pewter, china, fabrics, wallpaper, paint, locks, iron, and lighting fixtures, all faithful copies of old pieces in the Colonial Williamsburg Collection. Other appropriate items include paintings, books, needlework, and numerous articles

reminiscent of eighteenth-century Williamsburg. Catalogues are available, and a mail-order service is provided.

Williamsburg Lodge, Conference Center, and Auditorium—W.

This modern hotel of over 200 rooms has a dining room and coffeeshop. The Conference Center and Auditorium adjoining the Lodge are used for many Colonial Williamsburg educational activities and for other meetings. The Conference Center provides twelve meeting rooms, banquet and stage facilities, and a barber and beauty shop. The Lodge is owned and operated by the Colonial Williamsburg Foundation.

Abby Aldrich Rockefeller Folk Art Collection—E.

Adjacent to Williamsburg Inn and Craft House, this building houses the comprehensive collection of American folk art assembled by the late Mrs. John D. Rockefeller, Jr. The collection is displayed in nine exhibition rooms, designed as museum galleries but suggesting domestic interiors of the nineteenth century in which American folk art might have been hung originally. The building, designed in the style of early nineteenth-century architecture in America, makes use of Flemish bond brick-

work with stone trim and quoins. Over 1,500 examples of American folk art—oil paintings, watercolors, pastels, pen drawings, and wood and metal sculptures—are displayed in changing exhibitions. Visitors are admitted free of charge to the building. Scheduled gallery talks are provided, but visitors may go through the galleries at their own pace. Catalogues, facsimile reproductions, post cards, and greeting cards are available.

Waller Street—South to North

David Morton House and Shop—E.

David Morton, a Williamsburg tailor who either inherited wealth or acquired a lucrative trade, bought this property in 1777 from Benjamin Waller for £400. This sum indicates

that it probably included the house, which has now been reconstructed on the site, the adjacent small office, where Morton carried on his business, and the house next door, which he sold to Isham Goddin a year later. Accounts of a Williamsburg carpenter show that Morton made many repairs to the house, office, and dairy during his ownership. The shed portion at the rear of the dwelling was an addition. Archaeological investigations disclosed basement flooring just below ground level, indicating an English basement that probably was used as a kitchen and dining space. The railing at the front of the house reflects the popular Chinese influence. The wellhead is the focal point of a small garden planted in the eighteenth-century manner. Privately occupied.

Isham Goddin House—E.

Isham Goddin, a militiaman from nearby New Kent County before the Revolution, acquired this small house from his neighbor, David Morton, in 1778 for £200. Goddin later served on a committee concerned with the disposal of the property of Lord Dunmore, the last British royal governor, who fled Williamsburg for the security of a man-of-war in 1775. When Goddin returned to New Kent in 1783, he sold his plot and dwelling for only £90, reflecting the collapse in the value of real estate in Williamsburg when the capital was moved to Richmond. A distinctive feature of the reconstructed house is its central chimney. Privately occupied.

Christiana Campbell's Tavern—E.

Reconstructed. This long gambrel-roofed building has close associations with famous men and fine food, and is operated today as a restaurant by the Colonial Williamsburg Foundation in the spirit of its colonial proprietors. Specializing in assorted seafood dishes and steak, it stimulates the appetite as well as the historical imagination of present-day guests.

The original building on this site was known to be in service in 1765 as a tavern that offered accommodations and meals. An anonymous French traveler in that year proudly reported a visit here "where all the best people resorted," and where he soon struck up an acquaintance with many of them, "particularly with Colonel Burd."

In October 1765, on the eve of the enforcement of the Stamp Tax, this house figured in a dramatic episode. Colonel George Mercer, who had just been appointed distributor of stamps, arrived in town to be greeted by a mob of "gentlemen of property" and merchants. They pressed him to the porch of the building, where Governor Fauquier and some members of the Council were seated. Fauquier, well respected in Williamsburg, linked his arm in Mercer's and walked through a muttering crowd to the Palace, although his support was without effect because Mercer yielded to public pressure and declined the commission the next day.

In 1771 Mrs. Christiana Campbell, who had operated another tavern near the Capitol, moved her business here, bringing with her a distinguished patronage. For example, when George Washington came to town in the spring of 1772 to attend the House of Burgesses, he recorded in his diary that he dined here ten times within two months. Washington and his friends then had a "club" at Mrs. Campbell's, probably a private room set aside where they could gather for meat and drink and a discussion of everything from horse races to politics.

During the Revolution, Mrs. Campbell's was probably pressed into service on occasion to billet soldiers, as were neighboring taverns and ordinaries. When the Revolution was over and the capital had been removed to Richmond, business declined. In 1783 a young Scottish merchant from Yorktown, in Williamsburg with his new bride, was abruptly told that it was no longer "a house of entertainment"; prompted perhaps by this rebuff, he described Mrs. Campbell as "a little old Woman, about four feet high; and

equally thick," with "a little turn up Pug nose." Dining today is possible not only inside, but—when weather permits—on a landscaped terrace between the main house and the quarters at the rear.

The Blue Bell—W.

On this lot, granted in 1703 to John Redwood, keeper of the Public Gaol and caretaker of the Capitol, a large house was built sometime before 1707 and was operated as an ordinary. Purchased by Colonel Philip Ludwell the following year, it was owned by him and his heirs until 1832 and was rented to a variety of tenants. Thomas Bramer had a store here in which he carried wares ranging from delftware to molasses—an assortment typical of his trade and times. By 1768 the building had become known as the Blue Bell. Established by a archaeological findings, the most unusual feature of the reconstructed house is a kitchen in the basement instead of a separate building. A later shed-roof addition is represented at the rear. Privately occupied.

Powell's Tenement—W.

Once the shop of Peter Powell, wheelwright and riding-chair maker, this property (like the nearby Blue Bell) was acquired in 1708 by the prominent Ludwell family of nearby Green Spring plantation. It was rented in 1755 to Powell, who advertised the next year for an assistant, a blacksmith "who understands doing riding chair work." In 1779 the lot, then the property by inheritance of Lucy Lud-

liamsburg architecture. Its distinctive dusky brown color was also familiar to early residents. Most houses in the capital were painted white, but there is evidence of the various shades of brown, red, green, and blue that to-day's visitor observes. Elizabeth Carlos, a milliner and mantuamaker, owned this property from 1772 until 1777. In 1773, either lonely or pressed by creditors, she rented the house or a part of it to Mary Dickinson, another of the city's milliners. Privately occupied.

well Paradise, was confiscated by the Commonwealth of Virginia as Tory property, after "twelve good and reputable citizens" testified that the owner was living in England as a subject of the king. At that time the dwelling was occupied by the gaoler; it was certainly convenient to his charge. The reconstructed building now houses the heating plant for the Capitol. Behind it is the Powell Kitchen, privately occupied.

Elizabeth Carlos House—E.

This reconstructed story-and-one-half frame dwelling is typical of Wil-

Powell-Waller House and Office—E.

This comfortable house was erected in the mid-eighteenth century. Later alterations have now been stripped

from the building. The house derives its name from Benjamin Waller, who owned a large tract of land in this area in 1749 but disposed of it only to have his family reacquire the property late in that century, and from Benjamin Powell, who purchased the site in 1763 and presumably built this house upon it shortly afterward. Powell, a carpenter who became a successful contractor, built the steeple of Bruton Parish Church in 1768. Three years later he undertook to construct the newly authorized mental hospital building for the sum of £1,070. His rise to prominence, which typified that of other able and ambitious craftsmen of the period, culminated in his appointment to serve with Peyton Randolph, George Wythe, Robert Carter Nicholas, and other men of similar standing on a committee to enforce the boycott of British trade under the Continental Association. Powell sold the property

in 1782. After changing hands several times, it was purchased by Benjamin Waller's son, who deeded it to his son, Dr. Robert Waller, in 1814. The small brick building next to the restored house probably served as the doctor's office. This site is used for Colonial Williamsburg's educational programs, where thousands of students are able to become involved in craft activities and in the use of the house itself to gain a better understanding about living in colonial Virginia.

York Street—West to East

George Jackson House and Shop—N.

This property was once owned by George Jackson, a patriotic merchant who risked his neck as well as his fortune during the Revolution. Upon the death of his daughter Sarah, in 1854, a rambling but graphic newspaper account lauded her as "the last survivor of a once numerous family—and the youngest child but

one of George Jackson, who died in Williamsburg sixty years ago—a patriot who, at a gloomy period of the American Revolution, chartered a vessel to Bermuda, and there secretly and at eminent peril of life, procured a supply of gun powder, with which he returned in safety to the Old Dominion, and placed in the possession of his then desponding country." Jackson acquired the property in 1773 or 1774, soon after he had moved to Williamsburg from Norfolk. He apparently joined together two buildings which then stood on the site. This accounts for the contrasting roof slopes and cornice lines in the present reconstructed dwelling. Jackson presumably used the eastern portion for his shop; the east wall of the house, unbroken by any window, would have given an efficient shelf area. Privately occupied.

Cogar Shop—N.

This small eighteenth-century house was originally built in King and Queen County. In 1947 the owner moved it to this location, putting it to use as an antique shop. Acquired since by Colonial Williamsburg, it is privately occupied.

Nicolson House—N.

Robert Nicolson, who built this gambrel-roofed house, was a tailor and merchant. The off-center entrance door testifies to two periods of construction, the eastern part about 1752 and the western a few years later. For several years thereafter

Nicolson took in lodgers. At one point he noted in the *Virginia Gazette* that "Gentlemen who attend the General Courts and Assembly may be accommodated with genteel lodgings and breakfast and good stabling for their horses." One frequent lodger was James Mercer, who drew up the will of Mary Washington, mother of George Washington.

Mercer was a member of the General Assembly and a delegate to the Continental Congress. Finally, in 1777, Nicolson informed those who "used to put up at his house" that he "has now entirely discontinued taking in lodgers."

Nicolson initially had his shop across the street from his residence, and there his eldest son, William, joined him in the tailoring business. After a few years they opened a shop and store on Duke of Gloucester Street. Now designated as the Nicolson Shop, it was a much better location for commercial purposes. He sold the shop to William in 1779, but continued as a tailor and merchant.

Nicolson was prominent in civic affairs, serving on one pre-Revolutionary committee with such prominent fellow citizens as George Wythe, Peyton Randolph, and Robert Carter Nicholas. He was appointed in 1775 an agent for the Gun Manufactory in Fredericksburg to receive old brass much needed to provide arms for Virginia troops. He also performed wartime services as a tailor and merchant for the Publick Store located in Williamsburg, and in 1783 he was listed as a tax collector for the city. His son Robert became a doctor and settled in Yorktown, and another son, George, twice served as mayor of Richmond.

The residence, partially restored, is privately occupied.

CARTER'S GROVE

Carter's Grove is a James River plantation six miles southeast of Williamsburg on U. S. Route 60. It is owned by the Colonial Williamsburg Foundation. The plantation house and gardens are open to visitors.

Shaded by a row of enormous old tulip poplars, the Georgian mansion looks from high ground toward the river a quarter of a mile away. It is made up of five sections and stretches just over 200 feet from end to end. Perhaps built in the mid-1700s, the kitchen, at the eastern extremity, is the oldest part; the office, at the end of the western wing, was erected next; the main house in the center began to take shape in 1750 and was finished five years later; the connection between house and kitchen was built in 1907; and the other connecting structure was completed by 1930.

The 790 acres or so that now comprise the estate are part of the original 1,400-acre tract bought by Robert "King" Carter for the benefit of his daughter Elizabeth. "King" Carter—

so-called because of his princely possessions or his haughty ways, or perhaps for both reasons—was the progenitor of a large, wealthy, and influential clan in Virginia. At his death he was said to have been the owner of 300,000 acres of land, 1,000 slaves, and £10,000. His will specified that this particular plantation should pass to Elizabeth's son Carter Burwell, and that it "in all times to come be called and to go by the name of Carter's Grove."

Carter Burwell built the main house, hiring brickmasons and carpenters well known in Williamsburg, purchasing oyster shells for lime, and buying as well as making brick at the site. In 1752 Burwell paid the passage to America of a English artisan, Richard Baylis, and his family. For three years this skilled craftsman worked and supervised the work of others in carving and installing the magnificent woodwork that is the pride of Carter's Grove.

Carter Burwell died less than a

year after the house was completed. The plantation then passed from generation to generation of Burwells until 1838, when Philip Lewis Carter Burwell sold it to Thomas Wynne. Through the following ninety years Carter's Grove had a series of owners and tenants, some of whom did not or could not afford to maintain it properly. In 1928 Mr. and Mrs. Archibald M. McCrea purchased the property and, with the help of Richmond architect W. Duncan Lee, renovated and enlarged the house.

So skillfully was this work done that visitors find it hard to see where the changes were made. Briefly, the roof ridge of the main house was raised and dormer windows were added in order to make a livable third floor; the river-front walls of the kitchen and office dependencies and of the kitchen connector were set forward several feet and their roofs and second floors remodeled accordingly; and the office connector was built

with dimensions to balance the whole composition. Today the house and its furnishings, which date from the eighteenth, nineteenth, and twentieth centuries, are very much as they were left by Mrs. McCrea, who died in 1960. Both inside and out, Carter's Grove seems to merit its reputation as "the most beautiful house in America."

Aided by archaeological investigations, the development of gardens below the terrace to the south of the house is a continuing project. Future development of the plantation has already begun with the installation of an apple orchard containing six varieties grown in the tidewater area in the eighteenth century. Vegetables, field crops, and livestock known in the colonial period and a number of domestic craft activities will complete the recreation of the environment of an eighteenth-century working plantation at Carter's Grove.

INDEX

The chief descriptive entry for each building is
indicated by page numbers in boldface type.